THE BLACK PATH

Tariqa Azzeddini - Algiers

THE BLACK PATH

© Copyright Martinet Press (2015)

First edition 2015

ISBN-13: 978-0692484463

ISBN-10: 0692484469

All rights reserved. No part of this work may be copied or reproduced in any way without the expression written permission of the author and the publisher.

$$\text{فَأُمُّهُ هَاوِيَةٌ}$$

Their Mother is the Absolute.

THE BLACK PATH

TABLE OF CONTENTS

Introduction — 7

Chapter One: Origins — 31

Chapter Two: Instructions — 55

Chapter Three: Practices — 95

Chapter Four: Revelations — 155

Contact — 164

THE BLACK PATH

INTRODUCTION

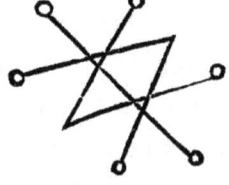

THE BLACK PATH

The Black Path begins in the desert.

The desert is a strange and terrible place. By day it's hotter than any place on earth, but at night it becomes colder than you would imagine. The sand doesn't hold the heat, and so it all rises into the sky. The foreign military companies that train there learn very quickly that you need to cover during the day to ward off the sun and keep your moisture inside, but you cover at night so that you don't catch hypothermia. The desert is a mystic place, where strange and unfamiliar things can appear to people, especially those who travel alone. Many times when I was with the French forces in Algeria, units who came back from night patrol would reluctantly report having seen some very bizarre apparitions, causing the officers to grimace and hurry the report along towards more mundane logistics. My own military detachment spent most of its time near the Algerian south, and I cannot claim that I liked the country very much. Algiers itself isn't bad as a city, but the Algerians don't like foreigners – and they really hate foreign soldiers. They're decent people and I don't blame them for hating the French, especially when you read some of the old records from the colonial period. Horrible stuff – rape, vandalism, pollution of holy places. People have their pride, and no one likes having their daughters turned into whores for the amusement of unwelcome mercenaries. Of course, it's a lot better today and the Algerians are back in charge of their own country, but those old memories are not going away anytime soon.

But whether the Arabs like you or hate you, at least in Algiers they're polite to you. They want your money, and so they smile and speak softly, and so there's a general kind of peace. It's not an international city, but there's a few thousand French expatriates there, and so people are used to the presence of off-duty soldiers. But south of Algiers things are more complicated; foreigners are not normally present except at the oil rigs, and the people are more cautious, even hostile towards strangers. Those people have seen too much war, too much blood, to be trusting or welcoming.

The only people who seemed at home in the South among the sand dunes are the Taoureg tribes of the desert, and the ragged clusters of Sufis who inhabited the ksars and *kasbah*s found near the lonely oases. The Taoureg are sometimes called the 'blue men', as they wander about with no apparent homes except the tents they carry with them. Some of the tribes have livestock that they drive from oasis to oasis seeking grazing space and water; other tribes are traders, bearing cargo across the Sahara desert. Many of the tribes were on the verge of starvation, until a substantial rise in contraband trafficking after the rise of Al Qaeda and Boko Haram. So foreign soldiers (like me) were deployed by the Algerian government to try to apprehend the shipments of cocaine and firearms, which now crossed the desert on the swaying backs of camels. It was an impossible mission, but one that paid well, and it gave me a chance to see a new part of the world. But the Sufis were different from the Taoureg tribes, and they were genuinely a mystery. As far as I understood, they were recognized as some kind of Islamic order, sort of like how Dominicans and Jesuits are orders of Catholicism. Islam I always hated – it's a bitter, angry, patriarchal religion that is bound and determined to stay in the dark ages. But the Sufis seemed to be different than other Muslims. They had nothing, and they needed nothing. Their earthen compounds called *zaouia* are always open to the weary traveler, even to soldiers. Someone once said that they are a peaceful people, but that never seemed right to me. Sufis aren't peaceful, they're detached. They don't care about this world or its rules or its struggles, because they're living half the time in the spirit world.

When there was time off, we usually didn't want to stay in Algeria if it could be helped. Despite the availability of amusements in Algiers, we had collectively shed too much Algerian blood to feel anything close to relaxation. Fortunately for us, Algeria borders Tunisia. Tunisia is also an Arab state, but it's officially secular. The capital, Tunis, is really cosmopolitan, and the Tunisians are very decent people. More modern somehow, less tied to the past. They want to develop as a state, and so they've gotten really serious. No terrorism, no criminal groups, just a small little country trying to make its way on the edge of the greatest desert in the world. But as my unit were stationed further south of Tunis city, we would more often visit the smaller city of Nafta, which borders on the edge of the great salt lake, the Chott el Djerid.

THE BLACK PATH

Nafta is a strange place; it's a small town with just over twenty thousand people, and it's mostly small buildings built out of yellow-gray bricks. It's a desert city, so it comes alive at night, since by day Nafta just bakes in the sun.

What makes Nafta unique is the number of small Sufi societies that make their home there. Now if you visit anywhere in North Africa, you get a lot of very large Sufi groups or *tariqas*, like the Qadiriyya, the Boutchichiyya, the Tijaniyya, the Shadhiyya, and other well known names. In Algeria and Morocco, you also find some really deviant groups who are more African than Muslim, like the Aissaoui, the Gnaoui, and the Hamadcha. But at Nafta, you find many small diverse *zaouias*. Some of them are large urban centers belonging to the larger and more orthodox Sufi brotherhoods. But others are just single-celled huts inhabited by a lone *cheikh* (saint) with two or three younger disciples. Never one for religion, I didn't care much for visiting mosques, but these *zaouias* were very different. The saints who lived there were like nothing I'd been raised to expect. When you read of the desert fathers of Catholic tradition, you learn of these self-loathing anchorites who fasted and prayed and flagellated to the point of extreme self-mortification, all in what seems like some hopeless quest for visions and dreams of a god who seems to hate all flesh and all humanity. But here in Nafta, there was a different type of saint than those self-hating messianics. These Sufi saints had a certain elegance to them, reserved, but noble.

Most of them were married and had women, children, and relations who lived at the *zaouia* alongside the disciples. The few saints I met were not starving madmen, but rather they seemed like sultans over their own small kingdom. I don't mean that the *zaouias* were especially luxurious (in fact it was the contrary), but rather that each *cheikh* seemed to possess an absolute awareness of themselves and their domain. When you met with one of these desert saints and looked them in the eye, you had no illusions that you were speaking to anything less than a kind of spiritual royalty. Their gaze was calm but unwavering, and they had absolutely no equals except another Sufi master, and it was rare that one *cheikh* would visit another. The atmosphere around them was charged with a certain energy that one does not feel in a mosque or church, I can only describe it as *otherworldly*. In many ways, it felt more like meeting a witch or sorcerer from some medieval tale – or maybe closer to home, a West African *bokkor* or shaman.

In Nafta, you see 'Muslim' practices that are completely foreign to mainstream Islam. In fact, those practices are alien to most forms of organized religion today. A French tour guide told me that much of these practices were brought into Tunisia from West Africa, and that if you spent time in Senegal or Mali, you'd see very similar rites among the traditional African movements, which later were watered down into Voudou and Candomble. Most of the *zaouias* in North Africa engage in practices that lead to trance states, but in the Maghreb (Algeria, Morocco, Tunisia) those trance states are very ecstatic, even aggressive. These trance states not infrequently lead to possession by the local *djinn* (spirits), or even by the *shayatin* (devils) in exceptional cases.

When the Sufis are in this wild ecstasy or possession, they are capable of remarkable behavior. An extreme yet memorable example: I personally witnessed a large group of entranced mystics swallowing broken glass and razor blades without any apparent injury at an Aissaoua lodge, and saw those same men the next day, none the worse for wear. And while most of the ceremonies were open to visitors, on several occasions when the trance grew wild, the foreigners were quickly ushered out of the *zaouia* by a resident *mokaddeme* (lodge master) to ensure that we were not attacked by frenzied devotees.

Over the four years that my unit was stationed in Algeria, I made several trips to Tunis, but more often I found that my heart was drawn to Nafta. When I couldn't get to Nafta, then I would increasingly visit the Sufi *zaouias* in Algeria, which were equally enchanting but less open to outsiders. I never visited any mosques, except sometimes late at night when they were empty, mainly because the daylight company of the Muslims remained distasteful to me. But the *zaouias* remained somehow the site of spiritual intrigue. By day, they were places of eerie calm; by night, they were places of hidden spiritual secrets. I'd been coming to Nafta for two years when Sidi Noureddine, the elderly owner of my habitual *riad* (guesthouse), suggested on the following night my visiting a particular *zaouia* just outside the city, near the edge of the Chott el Djerid salt lake.

I knew that my host was loosely affiliated with the Aissaoua brotherhood, and he had sent me with one of his sons to visit several of the local lodges. The occasion was a special *moussem* or festival for Sidi Ben Aissa (the Aissaoua founder), and Sidi Noureddine promised that there would be an excellent ceremony with much *baraka* (spiritual blessing) for all those who attended. He insisted strongly, and I was happy to visit a new lodge, especially if his boy was along to facilitate my attendance. If I was fortunate, I might even receive an audience with Cheikh Azzeddine, who was said to be a *wali'allah* or genuine living saint. The prospect of attending a *moussem* was exciting, and so I readily agreed.

So the following night I was driven to a moderate sized *kasbah*, and as we had departed the hotel somewhat late, we found the *moussem* already under way. The air was thick with the strong smell of incense, smoke and sweat, so much so that it stung my eyes. Following my guide, I made my way into the structure, a low two-floored building made of the same local earthen bricks. The main structure was wide and spacious, with an upper gallery looking inward. As was tradition in most of the local *zaouias*, the men occupied the ground floor, and the women looked on from the balconies and windows on the upper floor. The room was packed full of Sufis, and at the far end of the room, I could see the *cheikh* sitting cross-legged at the far end of the lodge, his closest disciples crouching around him in a tight circle, with other less favored devotees trying to get close enough to reach the *cheikh* or be blessed by him. My guide and I managed to find a space to sit down along one of the earthen walls of the courtyard, in tight quarters but comfortable enough. The room was filled with the banging of leather-hide drums and the occasional ear-shattering blasts of brass horns. Women and girls wailed from the balconies overhead, and the men on the ground floor all swayed back and forth in time while they chanted in unison. Several of the male *murids* (devotees) had worked themselves into a deep trance, and had staggered to their feet, and were beginning to flail about while snarling and growling, indicating that they were being 'ridden' by some of the *djinn* spirits who were being called on to attend the ceremony.

At the time I knew barely any Arabic, so my guide had to translate the liturgy for me into French (which he spoke well), and this was complicated as the room was so loud that he had to literally shout into my ear to be heard. My memory of the event is hazy due to the sheer sensory overload, but what I can recall from the ceremony is that at a certain point, a large black ram was brought into the hall, and a large black tarp was rolled out to cover the floor mats. The ram was struggling to get free, obviously in distress at the noise and the smells of the festival. Three of the *murids* flipped the thing onto its back, and a hush fell over the crowd. The *cheikh* rose from his seat, and moved to the animal. A long curved knife was passed to him, and he knelt over the animal, brandishing the blade over the throat of the ram. He carefully laid a hand on the head of the beast to steady it, and began to intone a loud invocation in Arabic.

Then the knife flashed, and a spurt of red splashed down on the tarp as the ram's head jerked and the legs kicked in the air. A hundred throats in the room began to groan, almost a growl, and there was a sense of something stirring on a very primal level.

My head began to spin, as if with motion sickness. Then before I could blink, those *murids* who had been worked into a frenzy fell upon the ram, grabbing its legs and pulling, pulling hard. A woman began to ululate on the upper floor, and the chanting resumed on the ground level. The frenzied *murids* started screaming and roaring, like apes or baboons, and then the ram was torn apart before my eyes. The carcass was strung up, and some began to eat the raw flesh, others began to pull out the organs and pass these around the throng, as if some bloody sacrament.

Some of the *murids* started cheering then, and the *cheikh* turned to return to his seat, holding the bloody knife aloft for all to see, as if evidence of the sacrifice. As he turned, though, my eyes met his, and I froze against my will. His dark eyes were quite piercing, and the weight of his eyes made my skin crawl. The sensation was rather not dissimilar to the kind of thrill one gets from watching a good horror film – one feels scared, but at the same time, one needs to know the object of terror. I felt exactly like that: this man had a quality that was really unnerving. Part of me was saying 'go, run, get out of here', but another part clawed at me from the inside to reach out to him and to get his attention. Between the blood, the incense, and the chanting, I could tell that my stomach was about to give way. Ingloriously I lurched to my feet and somehow managed to get outside. To my shame, even the fresh night air did not help enough, and I voided the contents of my stomach onto the desert sands outside the *zaouia* entryway.

My guide took me home afterwards, concerned that maybe he'd erred in bringing a *nasrani* (Christian foreigner) to such an event. I felt horribly embarrassed and was sure I'd never be invited back to any of the local *zaouias*, and so in the morning I packed my bags and prepared to return to Algiers. But when I tried to check out of the *riad*, my host (Sidi Noureddine) told me that one of the *murids* of Cheikh Azzeddine had called after the dawn prayer, and had insisted that I return to the *zaouia* to meet the saint. Apparently I was the first foreigner to have visited the lodge, and Cheikh Azzeddine wanted very much to receive me for tea and show proper hospitality, for which the Arabs are duly famous. I was embarrassed to return, but more afraid of giving offence to the Cheikh or to the kind owner of the *riad*, and so once more I made the trip by car to the lonely little *Kasbah* near the salt lake.

When we arrived, I was ushered into the same large room in which we'd been the night before. The black tarp had been rolled away, and the fog of incense and smoke had largely dissipated. I found Cheikh Azzeddine seated in the same spot as before, which I could see now was on a large flat cushion that rested atop the many rugs that covered the floor of the room. He was alone except for two of his *murids*, and appeared to be deep in conversation with them. As we entered the room, the Cheikh rose to his feet and came to greet us. He extended his hand as if to shake, and my host took the hand of the Cheikh and pressed his lips to it repeatedly.

I had seen this custom before in Algeria, as a gesture of profound respect. Then the Cheikh turned to me and took my hand, and shook it in the manner of the Europeans. I had expected him to be ancient, but on inspection he could not have been more than fifty, and he had a tanned but handsome face.

He wore a dark grey jellaba robe that one sees in most North African countries, with the hood down. His head was tied in a dark turban, tightly wound, so I could not tell the color of his hair (and I learned later that his head was shaved). The Cheikh had dark brown eyes, which reflected the light. He spoke in very slow French, in a rich and mellow voice, and he gave me the impression that he had studied French in the past, but did not use it much. He bid me to sit with him and take some tea (I did), and he was entirely curious about my career in the military, and my impressions of Algeria and Tunisia. He was extremely polite, and stared at me in a manner not dissimilar to how a lion stares at its prey. I had the very distinct impression that I was face-to-face with a great predator, but also a very holy man. It was entirely unnerving, and I found myself almost paralyzed while in his company.

Soon the conversation turned to religion, and this was no great surprise. The Cheikh asked if I was Christian, and I replied that I did not consider myself such.

He asked if I was Muslim, and I answered (with some embarrassment) that I'd seen very little in my travels that made me want to be a follower of Islam. He smiled a little at my answer, and then asked what I thought of Sufism. Carefully (as I felt it very important to make a good impression on him), I told him how I'd spent the last two years in Algeria and Tunisia visiting different *zaouia*, and that I felt very much at peace when I visited such lodges. He nodded, then he asked me how I felt about the ritual I had observed the night before. Knowing that he must have known that I'd had to leave suddenly, I told him as plainly as I could that I'd found the rite incredibly exciting and moving on some primitive level, but that fatigue and illness had gotten the better of me. This answer did not seem to especially please him or displease him, and rather than reply, he proceeded to simply stare at me as if expecting more. Cheikh Azzeddine waited patiently while I tried to think of something intelligent or clever to say, but with him staring at me, I felt helpless to carry on anything like the usual polite conversation. Finally, sensing that his patience would soon wane, I blurted out that I needed his help. He seemed to expect the question, and said he could help me, by showing me what I had been searching for: **the Black Path**.

My knowledge of religion was minimal, so I had never heard of such a thing. I asked him what the Black Path was, and he smiled. He said that to answer that, he would tell me a story.

THE BLACK PATH

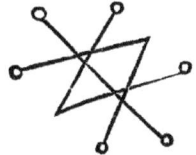

Years ago, Azzeddine had come into contact with the Aissaoua brotherhood in Algiers, where he had been sent to study engineering. His home town in southern Algeria was a poor village of less than one hundred inhabitants, and his family were mostly poor and illiterate. He had himself never been a great Muslim, and preferred to spend time 'raising hell' and carousing with friends rather than at prayers. But by chance, he'd been invited to visit an Aissaoua *zaouia* during the holidays, and when the rites of *hadra* (ecstasy) had begun, he had made the serious mistake of mocking the *murids* and mimicking some of their ecstatic practices, to the amusement of his friends. At that point, he was seized by an angry *djinn* and underwent a very violent possession. While others there chanted the names of Allah and danced wildly, the young engineer went into seizures and cavorted wildly, laughing and baying like a *d'bah sahraoui* (the desert hyena). When several *murids* tried to restrain him, he had thrown them off and bitten one quite badly. The *mokaddeme* of the *zaouia* had not been able to expel the *djinn*, and Azzeddine had to be removed by force. When the young engineer regained control of his senses, he was alarmed to learn that he'd bitten one of the *murids* and that he'd disrupted the ceremonies. He was taken home, exhausted, but his spiritual misfortunes had only just begun.

For several nights, he struggled with fever and delirium, and eventually a doctor was called – but there was no evidence of disease or sickness. Eventually his parents were able to obtain a visit from another Sufi saint, of the somewhat more orthodox Rahmaniyya lineage. The saint struggled for several hours with the *djinn*, and attempted all the traditional *ruqiyyah* arts of Quranic recitation and application of certain oils. But the *djinn* was undaunted, and insulted the old saint, claiming that Azzeddine was its lawful property, and that he was a wicked sinner besides. After two days of this spiritual battle, the old *cheikh* was growing alarmed – either the *djinn* was quite powerful, or else his own spiritual powers were failing. Neither would it release the young engineer, nor would it even give up its own name, so that the *cheikh* could command it. In desperation, the *cheikh* tried a different approach: was there something the *djinn* would accept in order to leave? The evil spirit replied that it would not be pacified unless Azzeddine made a pilgrimage to the *Kaf el-Jnoun* (Cave of the Jinn) on the border of Algeria and Libya, and that the young man should spend a night on the summit in prayer. The saint reluctantly agreed to this demand, and vowed that the journey would be made. The *djinn* announced that it would not release Azzeddine until this was done, but it would cease to torment the young man for the moment.

THE BLACK PATH

The fever receded and the delirium began to subside. The Rahmaniyya saint admonished him for having attended the wild rites of the Aissaoua, and warned Azzeddine against attending their ceremonies or houses in the future. The young engineer listened to him politely, but refused to make the journey to the place specified by the *djinn*. The Kaf el-Jnoun was an infamous mountainous region that was widely known in folklore as one of the doorways to the underworld, and it was not visited (let alone climbed) by Arabs – only the French were considered to be bold or stupid enough to try. But the saint insisted that he would become much sicker than before if he reneged on his promise to the Jinn. So reluctantly, the young engineer agreed to make the pilgrimage, and the next two days were spent in hasty preparation for the journey.

THE BLACK PATH

Cheikh Azzeddine did not speak much about the journey to the mountain. Several of his friends had gone with him, but they refused entirely to join him on the climb, and in fact tried to dissuade him from making the effort. But Azzeddine could feel the evil spirit coiled inside (he said), and made the climb alone. He said little to me about the climb, only that it was bitterly hot, even by Algerian standards, but that it became extremely cold after dark.

That night, the young engineer expected to be freed of the evil spirit, but it was not to be. There, in the absolute emptiness of the desert, and in that cursed place, the *djinn* awoke to new fury within him. The Cheikh admits that he remembers very little of the ten or so hours that he spent on the summit, as he was wracked with terrible convulsions. He bit his own wrists and lapped up his own blood when it flowed. He howled at the moon and stars, certainly terrifying his friends below and any desert travelers that may have been abroad. He soiled himself repeatedly, which he admitted calmly and without embarrassment. Finally the seizures began to subside. Where previously he had felt the presence of the *djinn* like a kind of hostile intruder, now he felt a particular unity of being with the alien consciousness, as if it had somehow been integrated within him on some visceral level. The seizures had left him weakened, yet strangely invigorated. The taste of blood in his mouth and the bile staining his clothes should have been repulsive, but he simply did not care. Then his mind opened, and he *saw*.

THE BLACK PATH

Our own universe dissolved into insignificance, breaking down into its subtle parts. Beyond this world, he saw a vision of two paths. One path was bright, leading to a white tree in the middle of a great city of shining gold. The other path was dark, and it lead to a black tree in the middle of a great black city. At the intersection of the two paths was a towering figure, wreathed in flames. Intuitively, Azzeddine understood that this was the evil spirit which possessed him. Then the entity spoke to him in a clear voice for the first time, and told Azzeddine that he had been chosen, chosen to reveal a great teaching that would impact many lives. It revealed itself to him as Azazel. This was unnerving for the young engineer, as Azazel is the true name of the devil in Islamic tradition. The spirit told him that he must choose between two paths: one leading to the Light, and the other to the Darkness. It spoke blasphemous words of an ancient war before time, a struggle between the primordial darkness and usurping light, of stolen origins and humanity cheated and trapped even before its creation. The spirit cursed Allah and His angels, and promised a terrible vengeance against the prophets who had denied the truth, leading their people instead into spiritual slavery to a god who hates them. And it spoke of a coming savior, the *Dajjal*, who would cleanse the earth of Islam and other false religions, and return humanity to the worship of the Absolute. Azzeddine was meant to prepare the way, as a crier in the desert. He would return to Algeria and begin to teach others the truth. But he must choose the black path, and forever forsake any hope of Ferdous (Paradise). He would go down to the Black City and eat of the forbidden Zaqqum tree. But first, he must put his trust in Azazel, and then he would be shown things that were known only to saints.

Cheikh Azzeddine had been torn – such things are warned against in Islam. Evil spirits are known to tempt and deceive, but the words of this spirit burned into his mind. Steeling himself, he had pledged himself to Azazel and asked to be shown the black path. The burning spirit seized him and pressed its flaming mouth to his. Then spirit breathed into him and his lungs were scorched and burned with fire, the spirit communicated to him the Secret – the terrible, unspeakable truth. The Secret changed him into a saint, and he had returned from the mountain as a man transformed. He left the school of engineering and took up residence in a *zaouia* in southern Algeria, and eventually had been invited by his small group of followers to move to Nafta. His community was small, but the *Dajjal* did not require many disciples, only a dedicated few.

The Cheikh did not speak at length about the Secret. He said that he could not explain it to me or describe it to me in any human words. But if I too wanted to know the Truth about this world, and the hidden war that is being waged daily, he was willing to share the Secret. If I was willing to leave behind the world and its false gods of materialism and secularism, and to pledge myself to his teachings, he would welcome me into the fraternity. I asked him about the black path, and he said it is lit with hellfire, which burns away the weakness and false ego of humanity, transmuting the human from clay into smokeless fire.[1] Looking into the eyes of Cheikh Azzeddine, I could see those flames burning. This holy man seemed more a terrible angel given flesh than a mere human, and no one had ever terrified me or fascinated me as he did.

I have never liked religion. I hate the hypocrisy and morality, and lies and ethical codes that change every year to line up with whatever form of social justice is in vogue. Most religious leaders are obvious frauds with no real answers, and they are often as vicious and political as normal human politicians. I hate the idea of a deity that gives people instincts to fuck and fight, and then chortles while threatening to put them into an eternal crematorium for not respecting him. But that was not what this *cheikh* seemed to be offering me. I had the very keen feeling that to accept this man as my teacher would be to accept a new spirit, a real baptism by fire that would transform me into something more than human.

---

[1] In Islamic tradition, hellfire is said to be black as pitch, and thick like tar.

Of course, I accepted. And over the next three years, I spent increasing amounts of time in Nafta. When Cheikh Azzeddine decided to relocate back to southern Algeria, he asked me in turn to begin to collect his teachings and prepare them for publishable form. This book is my humble effort to collate his practices and beliefs into a single coherent narrative. This is important firstly, because while my spiritual master still identifies as a member of the Aissaoua tradition, his understanding of the tradition is unique to him. Secondly, there is very little of the Aissaoua *tariqa* in modern English, though there is more in French if you can read it. Finally, Cheikh Azzeddine hopes that through the publication of this text, people outside of North Africa will become better aware of the rich spiritual practices of the dark continent. Much of what is written here will be offensive to many of the People of the Book (Jews, Christians, Muslims), but Cheikh Azzeddine says that in this day, spiritual warfare is best fought with the pen. If even five or six people read this work and decide that the Black Path is for them, then it will be enough.

I wish you all success in your own spiritual journey. May the blessings of my *cheikh* and his own spiritual masters be with you as you read this book.

Marcel Montaigne
Zaouia Az-Zaqqum, Algiers

CHAPTER ONE: ORIGINS

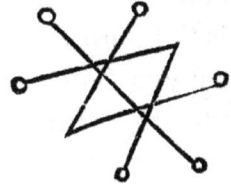

The Aissaoua *Tariqa*

For four centuries, the Aissaoua society has been the object of both fascination and dread. It appeared first in North Africa in the 15th century with its founder, Cheikh Mohamed al-Hadi ben Aissa. But unlike other Sufi traditions, the Aissaoua *tariqa* has never been accepted as a normal Sufi movement. Sufism had already been in Africa since the medieval period, and was characterized by its sober spiritual practices, such as chanting the Quran, prayers, and fasting. Yet the tradition founded by Cheikh ben Aissa had none of these characteristics. Ben Aissa claimed that his Sufi *tariqa* was an extension of the Shadhiliyya and Jazuliyya Sufi lodges into which he himself had been initiated. It used some of the same prayers and invocations, and borrowed many of the Sufi manuals and handbooks for study. But here ended any obvious similarity to orthodox Sufism, let alone Islam. Cheikh bin Aissa began to incorporate the performance of certain traditional African practices, which were condemned by the Muslim scholars as profane and non-Islamic. His students were said to speak to the *djinn* (spirits), and to even take them as wives and concubines. People who visited the Aissaoua *zaouias* found them operating largely at night, which was held to be inauspicious and disreputable. The Aissaoua engaged in wild, frenzied trances, which sometimes lead to states of possession by the *djinn* or *shayatin* (devils). Cheikh ben Aissa is said to have been a masterful scholar of Quran and the Islamic sciences, and for this reason he was himself widely respected by other Islamic scholars despite the odd reputation of his new esoteric society. However, his students also studied profane texts like the *Ghayat-ul-Hakim* (the Picatrix), and occupied themselves as mediums and sooth-sayers. When other Sufi *cheikh*s went to visit the lodge centers of the Aissaoua movement, they were horrified to see that the devotees were even practicing extreme self-mutilation as evidence of their spiritual advancement. Yet the membership of the Aissaoua fraternity seemed to be pious Muslims, despite their unorthodox practices, and as Cheikh Ben Aissa himself was widely hailed as a great spiritual master, the movement was allowed to continue. The great spiritual master continued to preach and teach until his death in 1526, and his tomb can be found today in the city of Miknes.

While the Muslim leadership were willing to turn a blind eye to the eccentric practices of the Aissaoua, the European colonial powers were less willing or able to do so. While the Aissaoua were reluctant to admit foreigners to their fraternity, some few were given privileged access to their secret ceremonies. Witnesses reported startling accounts of demonic possession, lycanthropy, and animal sacrifice by rending. Even the New York Times managed to get an especially lurid account of Aissaoua festivities, which it published in its edition of Feb 12, 1882. These foreign accounts are sometimes accused of a colonial bias, but they are consistent with documents in Arabic authored by Muslim authorities from the same period, and of those few academics who specialize in North African spiritual movements. Given the scandalous reports, the African states were compelled to repress the Aissaoua, and several of the prominent *zaouias* were shut down or forced to relocate. Yet almost four centuries after his death, Ben Aissa's *zaouias* can be found across the Maghreb region (Algeria, Morocco, Tunisia), and has gone into western Africa and Europe. The city of Meknes remains of special importance, as it is the cult center and burial place of Cheikh Ben Aissa.

The Aissaoua movement is disorganized, with little central authority. In the last century, several of the larger Aissaoua lodges have tried to claim primacy, but the movement lacks any genuine central authority. Most Aissaoua have taken an oath of fealty (*bay'ah*) to their own *cheikh*, who operates freely within his own particular lodge. While some lodges number in the hundreds, some are also very small, with only a handful of disciples clustered around a senior devotee, who may not himself even be a *cheikh*. Women are deeply involved in the movement, but usually as clients and patrons of the *cheikh*s. Given this lack of central authority, the practices of the Aissaoua vary greatly from one region to another. Where one *zaouia* will revere certain local *djinn*, another lodge will revere more 'universal' *djinn* spirits. Some *zaouias* practice animal sacrifice frequently, while others cannot afford to do so. Music, drumming, and trance states are important to almost all Aissaoua, but there are some lodges in urban centers that have had to suspend these practices to avoid confrontation with unsympathetic neighbors. The central belief structure of the mainstream Aissaoua is largely an African cosmology, with cosmetic Islamic influences overlaid. To be fair, the mainstream *zaouias* today take pains to appear more Muslim, and the African elements are entirely withheld from non-members in order to avoid scandal of any kind.

The core Aissaoua cosmology can be stated as follows:

1. The supreme deity (Allah) creates the universe and divides it into three worlds: the celestial, terrestrial, and infernal. Allah divides the three worlds into two parts: the exoteric (*dahir*) and esoteric (*batin* or *ghaib*).

2. The Throne of Allah is established in the esoteric part of the celestial world.

3. He next creates the angels out of light, and the *djinn* out of pure fire, then humanity out of clay.

4. Allah assigns the worlds to his creatures:

    - Celestial (esoteric): the prophets and saints
    - Celestial (exoteric): the angels and blessed dead

    - Terrestrial (esoteric): the *djinn*

- Terrestrial (exoteric): humanity

- Infernal (exoteric): the sinful dead
- Infernal (esoteric): devils, heretics.

5. Some *djinn* rebel under the chief *djinn* (Iblis). They are given respite to the Day of Judgment, when they shall be cast into the Infernal world (*Jahannam*). They harass angels, *djinns*, and humans whenever possible.

6. Humanity and *djinns* are given the choice to serve Allah and strive for Paradise, or else to merit eternal damnation.

The Two Paths (Religion & Esotericism)

The mainstream Aissaoua profess that there are two paths which lead to salvation from hellfire. These are *religion* and *esotericism*.

RELIGION: Through the religions of the Book (i.e. Judaism, Christianity, and Islam), Allah establishes a path where the sinner may labor with good deeds to attain the exoteric level of heaven. This path is uncertain, and the sinner struggles against their own animal nature for the entire journey. Human attributes likes lust, pride, and arrogance must be overcome with great effort. The sinner dies unsure of their own spiritual fate, and hope for mercy on the Day of Judgment. This is the path of most Muslims.

ESOTERICISM: The mainstream Aissaoua *tariqa* offers a different spiritual trajectory. Through the benediction of the spiritual master (the *cheikh*), the disciple (*murid*) can enter an alternate spiritual path with extreme practices. Through such taboo rites as ecstatic dancing, trance states, and possession, a *murid* can transform their inner spiritual weaknesses into spiritual strengths. Lust becomes Union with the Beloved. Wrath becomes Heroic Spirit. Arrogance is transformed into Divine Pride. These practices cannot be learned without a spiritual master, because they can be misapplied without the correct guidance. Through the Aissaoua path, the sinner dies fearless and confident of their arrival in the highest (esoteric) level of Heaven. While the practices of the Aissaoua are certainly extreme in comparison to other more mainstream Sufi groups, the essential conception of the two paths is the same.

The *murids* of the mainstream Aissaoua *tariqa* have chosen the second path (esotericism), and embark on a journey of intense self-discovery. This journey is undertaken with the close supervision of their *cheikh*, who usually develops an intimate connection with the *murid* over a period of years. The *cheikh* prescribes the same basic practices (*dhikr*, *wird*) for all disciples, and then assess the individual student's level much like a sports coach, so that he may indicate which spiritual exercises are best undertaken. A new disciple should not take on advanced exercises, or s/he may be driven insane or killed by possessing spirits. Advanced disciples must not be given only basic practices, or they will not make much progress and may be tempted to experiment on their own – or just find another *cheikh*. Many of the basic practices are indistinguishable from mainstream Sufism, such as lengthy prayers and readings of the Quran, and are designed to test the sincerity of the initiate. The African elements of the *tariqa* come into play later, as the *cheikh* works to slowly introduce the *murid* to the spirit world. It is held by the Aissaoua that since many human neuroses and sicknesses stem from spiritual problems, they must be treated by spiritual means. Likewise, it is also held that by increased contact with the spirit world, the spiritual body of the human is slowly transmuted into a higher being. This is not intended metaphorically, but taken as a literal (if secret) truth. Some *cheikh*s describe states of *ecstase* where their spirit leaves their body and is able to travel around like the *djinn*, and even interact with the material world in a limited capacity as if a *djinn*. More importantly, some Aissaoua believe that upon death, the spirit (*ruh*) of an accomplished *murid* may evade the angels of judgment, and simply ascend directly into the Celestial realms.

THE BLACK PATH
The Aissaoua–Azzeddini

The Sufi sect of Cheikh Azzeddine differs from its parent sect not in terms of its practices, but rather in its inverted cosmology. In fact, if one were to visit the main Aissaoua *zaouia* in Algiers during a *moussem*, and then to visit a smaller Azzeddini *zaouia* on the same night in the same city, one would likely see the same basic practices. This is complicated by the fact that the Azzeddini do not themselves care to differentiate themselves from the mother tradition, as the differences are largely philosophical. This is actually an oversimplification, but shows the strength of connections between the two branches of the tradition which traces its routes to Cheikh Ben Aissa. Also, the Azzeddini branch of the tradition is considerably smaller, with only five *zaouias* reported across Algeria, Morocco, Tunisia, and no formal *zaouias* outside of North Africa. Relations are strained mostly when a learned Aissaoui becomes aware of the distinctives of the Azzeddini rite, in which case they are likely to denounce the *zaouia* members as *zanadiq* (heretics) or worse, devil worshippers (*iblisiyya*). To be fair, this is not an unreasonable deduction, when one examines the theology of Cheikh Azzeddine.

Following his epiphany at Kaf-l-Jnoun, Cheikh Azzeddine outlined his radical cosmology as follows:

THE BLACK PATH

1. In the beginning, there is the Absolute (*Haawiya*). It encompasses all existence and non-existence. It is filled with primordial beings which are emanations (*Tawaghit*) of its nature, of which the foremost is the Shaitan.

2. Within the Absolute, a second entity arises known as The Light (*An-Nour*).

3. The Light attempts to conquer and subdue the Absolute. This proves impossible.

4. The Light emanates the Universe, to have its own kingdom.

5. The Light divides the Universe into the three worlds (Celestial, Terrestrial, and Infernal), which it further subdivides into two parts: the exoteric (*dahir*) and esoteric (*batin* or *ghaib*).

6. The Light establishes its throne in the esoteric part of the Celestial world.

7. The Light then creates seven chief angels (*As-Sebt*) out of light, which in turn create other angels. The Light then creates the *djinn* out of pure fire, then humanity out of clay. While the Light is the shaper of these sentient beings, their animating principle (*baraka*) comes originally from the Absolute.

8. The Light assigns the worlds to his creatures:

    - Celestial (esoteric): the prophets and saints
    - Celestial (exoteric): the angels and blessed dead

    - Terrestrial (esoteric): the *djinn*
    - Terrestrial (exoteric): humanity

    - Infernal (exoteric): the sinful dead
    - Infernal (esoteric): renegade *djinn*

9. The Shaitan seeks to reincorporate the Universe. To do so, the Absolute generates the Black City (*Jahannam*) as its cosmic bastion. It releases certain primordial spirits into the Universe as agents of its will.

10. Some angels rebel against the Light, and choose to serve the Absolute instead. These thereafter are termed *devils*.

11. Humanity and *djinns* must choose to serve either the Light or the Absolute. The Light offers ego-centric permanent bliss for servitude; the Shaitan offers reunification with the Absolute.

The Two Paths (Religion vs. Esotericism)

Like the larger Aissaoua tradition, the Azzeddini recognize two spiritual paths, though they are NOT held to be equal or similar in direction.

RELIGION: Cheikh Azzeddine maintains that religion is a construct of the Light, whether the Light is understood as the supreme deity of the Abrahamic religions, or the other revealed religions (Hinduism, Sabeans, Zardushti, etc.). Religion serves to shape the human into an effective slave of the deity. Through the practice of the prescribed prayers and rituals, the spirit (*ruh*) of the worshipper can become sufficiently attuned to the Celestial world, such that it will ascend to this region after death. Here, the worshipper enjoys the permanent bliss of the divine presence, and maintains their separate ego (*nafs*). If one accepts the cosmological model of the Azzeddini sect, this is tantamount to asking to be put into jail. The terrestrial world must be renounced (at least partially) in order to achieve the celestial world.

ESOTERICISM: The Azzeddini believe that the Absolute is the ultimate source of all being and non-being, and that reunification with the Absolute is the only possible escape from the trauma of existence. To achieve the knowledge and contact with the Absolute is very hard, as the Universe and its spiritual systems are heavily influenced by the Light. For this reason, the spiritual systems that point towards the Black City are characterized by antinomian behaviors and traumatic practices, which are designed to shock the spirit (*ruh*) free of the false ego (*nafs*). True spirituality is like surgery – it is sometimes painful, just as the physician's knife is necessarily painful. Ultimately the universe is also a reflection of the Absolute, and so it is not to be renounced, though it must be transcended.

Mainstream Aissaoua Practices

The most fundamental difference between the Aissaoua tradition and the other Sufi traditions is the emphasis on experience over learning. In other words, most of the major Sufi societies place great emphasis on the study of the written works of their founder, as well as other major Sufi masters. Most Sufi paths are very bookish, and at a certain level do require that the student memorize and be able to expound upon a small library of philosophy and metaphysics. However, all Aissaoua (regardless of sect) reject book learning or deep philosophy, as they consider these to be a waste of time. There is no armchair philosophy or endless speculation for those who take the Aissaoua path. Instead of reading books, the Aissaoua model of spiritual development forces the initiate to discover *ma'rifa* (esoteric knowledge) through deep self-knowledge, and contact with external spiritual entities. As mentioned earlier, the spiritual model developed by Cheikh Ben Aissa includes practices which are widely considered heretical by mainstream Muslim scholars, as it incorporates African spiritual elements. Most of these features are maintained by Cheikh Azzeddine. Prominent examples include the following:

ECSTATIC TRANCE: Today, most Sufi traditions employ altered states of consciousness as part of their daily spiritual practice. These states of consciousness are referred to usually as *hal* (pl. *ahwal*), which translates loosely as 'subtle trance'; the ritual used to induce it is referred to as *hadra* (trance ceremony). In mainstream Sufism this is achieved commonly through the repetition of the 99 divine names (*asma Allah el-husna*), which may be chanted thousands of times. Visitors to a *zaouia* will often see Sufis seated on the ground, slowly rocking back and forth while intoning *Allah! Allah! Allah!* or *Ya Nour! Ya Nour!* ('Oh Light, oh Light!'). Such practices will frequently induce a very gentle *hal* (trance) state, in which the Sufi will experience a dissociation from their physical body, and sensations of inner peace and bliss. This type of *hadra* is considered a fundamental practice, which is carried out by both neonates through to the most advanced *cheikh*s of the various traditions.

The Aissaoua do make use of subtle trances for their public rites, but this is not considered a typical Aissaoua practice. Rather, the Aissaoua chose instead to undergo such practices as drumming and dancing, in hopes of entering a wild, euphoric trance state referred to as *ecstase* (ecstasy). In many ways, this is similar to the type of mental state that is induced in the contemporary 'rave' scene, where intense rhythms, wild dance, and deep bass induce a type of atavistic trance in attendees. These practices are very similar to certain practices in West African spiritual traditions, from which they are almost certain to have been derived. The Azzeddini regularly engage in ecstatic trance states, as they believe that it liberates the spirit (*nafs*) from the mundane mind (*'aql*), and allows for heightened reception of esoteric knowledge (*ma'rifa*). Aissaoua devotees who are deep in *ecstase* (ecstasy) may learn to manifest their inner *wahsh* (beast), which tends to follow totemic lines. When an Aissaoua enters the deepest and most violent levels of *ecstase*, they may begin (e.g.) to growl like a lion or howl like a wolf or gorilla. This being the case, claims that the Aissaoua are a lycanthropic cult are not entirely wrong, and visitors are not normally encouraged to attend the wild trance rites, as the initiates experiencing *ecstase* may attack onlookers who are not involved in the rites – and will certainly attempt to savage anyone who mocks the proceedings. On days when a *moussem* (festival) involves a procession through a town, the *mokademme* of the *zaouia* must take special care to warn spectators away, as the ecstatic states have resulted in physical attacks on people who stray too close to the devotees, in a similar way to the reported Bacchanals of the Hellenistic Europe and North Africa. This is not considered possession per se, as this kind of trance state is purely an internal phenomena, which reveals the inner nature of the initiate instead of inviting external forces inside. The Azzeddini in particular consider the manifestation of the *wahsh* (beast) as a spiritual milestone, which demonstrates that the initiate has learned to suppress their mundane cognition in search of genuine divine awakening.

Self-mutilation is also another frequent practice during *ecstase*, and this aspect of Aissaoua is one of the most horrifying to outsiders, and consequently the most remarked upon. This can take many forms, though the most common is laceration with razors, sharp rocks, or knives. Piercing with nails and skewers is also common. Less common is burning. Some *zaouias* will also include the drinking of burning or boiling fluids, or even the ingestion of razor blades or broken glass. Islam strictly prohibits acts of self-cutting or self-piercing, indeed self-injury of any kind, and yet the Aissaoua consider this to be one of the best indicators of genuine spiritual development. The practice is considered one of the best tests of genuine *hal* (trance) or *ecstase*, as these feats of extreme endurance can only be undertaken by someone who is legitimately in a state of altered consciousness. If someone is attempting to simulate a trance state, even unconsciously, they will be caught out when they balk at committing these acts of self-mutilation. By contrast, an Aissaoua who is genuinely deep in *ecstase* will not hesitate to follow the instructions of the *cheikh* or *ma'llem* (teacher), no matter how gruesome the test.

The *zaouias* which are under the teaching of Cheikh Azzeddine make use of these mainstream Aissaoua trance states and techniques with only minor variation; the theoretical differences are mainly in the goals of the trance, which will be discussed below in Chapters Two and Three.

Engaging the Spirit World

Almost all Sufi traditions acknowledge that the terrestrial world has a physical (exoteric) dimension and an unseen spiritual (esoteric) dimension. Humans are native to the physical world, but are sensitive to the spiritual world to a greater or lesser degree. The *djinn*, by contrast, are native to the spiritual (esoteric) world, though they are also sensitive to the physical world to a greater or lesser degree. This duality of character leads sometimes to interaction and potentially conflict between the two worlds, especially when a particular human or *djinn* is particularly adept at perceiving or affecting their opposite dimension. As an example: both *djinn* and humans may inhabit a particular structure. When a human accidentally manipulates the spiritual form of a house, it can alarm or anger the *djinn*. When the *djinn* deliberately or accidentally manipulates the physical dimension of a house, we say it is 'haunted' (*maskun*). When a human attempts to coerce the *djinn* into performing whatever action, the act is called 'sorcery' (*sihr*). When a *djinn* attempts to coerce a human, the human is said to be 'possessed' (*majnun*).

Due to their spiritual practices, Sufi masters are expected to be somewhat conversant with both planes of existence. This being the case, when a place or person is thought to be under malignant influence by a hostile spirit, a *cheikh* is called to perform *ruqiya* (exorcism) through the reading of the Quran and related practices. Most frequently the spirits in question are elemental beings (*djinn*), or else more inhuman and violent spirits like the *ghul* or *afreet*. Interaction with the dead is almost entirely unknown in Muslim esotericism. In most Sufi traditions, possession is seen as inconvenient at best and life-threatening at worst.

The Aissaoua differ from the other Sufi groups in that they actively pursue possession as a legitimate spiritual practice. A mainstream Aissaoua *cheikh/ma'llem* will anticipate working together with benign *djinn*, and to ask their help (when necessary) against the malevolent *djinn* and *shayatin*. In the private ceremonies, both initiates of the order and their clientele engage in ecstatic trance states, inviting particular spirits to join in the ritual and to possess the person in question. This process must be handled with extraordinary care, and requires the following considerations:

1. First (and most critically) a qualified spiritual master must be present to oversee the ceremonies. This master of ceremonies may be a *cheikh* or else a *ma'llem* (master) who is authorized by the *cheikh* to organize such rites.

2. Second, the candidate for possession must be examined by the *cheikh/ma'llem*. Is the person of unsound body and mind? Are they currently under

a spell or enchantment by an enemy, which might complicate the possession? Have they somehow angered their *qarina* (*djinn* twin)? If so, possession by even a benign spirit may harm the spiritual seeker, and anger the spirits involved.

3. Third, the spiritual needs of the candidate for possession must be understood. Is the candidate another Aissaoua? Are they seeking possession for spiritual advancement and to achieve *ma'rifa* (esoteric knowledge)? Is the purpose of the rite to have an Aissaoua serve as an oracle? Or is the candidate a client who seeks spiritual medicine or relief from some curse?

4. Fourth, the *cheikh/ma'llem* must have sufficient spiritual insight to perceive what spirits are available to assist, and if their price can be met. As the Aissaoua are a very local tradition, the *cheikh/ma'llem* must give consideration to which spiritual powers lay claim to an area. If the *Lila* (ceremony) is performed in Meknes, the spiritual powers will not be the same as those spiritual powers in Bou Saada or Nafta.

5. Fifth, and finally, the *cheikh/ma'llem* must also know if they themselves are sufficiently advanced to deal with the spirits to be invoked / evoked. If the spirit is a mild *djinn*, all is well and good. If instead it is a vicious *afreet*, then the *cheikh/ma'llem* must have other disciples on hand to restrain the majnoun (possessed

one), and to assist with the ceremony if things get out of hand. Once the particular spirits have been identified, the *cheikh/ma'llem* must consider the specifics of the spirits involved. If the *djinn* is known to local lore, there are likely to be specific gifts which it will expect for its assistance, like flowers and scarves of specific color, or blood sacrifices of particular animals. The *djinn* are known to be very carnal beings (despite the spiritual composition), and frequently insist on a 'marriage' with the initiate. This may be a short-term marriage or a permanent marriage, and each will involve a certain number of taboos or stipulations that the spirit will expect. The infamous succubus Aicha Kandicha is known to demand marriage from men she helps, but she is famous for draining her 'husbands' of their vitality during her nightly conjugal visits, sometimes resulting in insanity or death.

As Western tourism has become increasingly interesting in access to the 'forbidden séances' of the Aissaoua, there has been increasing pressure on the Aissaoua lodges to perform ceremonies in exchange for 'donations' or 'gifts' from the audience. This has lead to simulated ceremonies that lack the sacred elements which are not suited to the eyes of the uninitiated. Visitors to an Aissaaoua *Lila* (night ceremony) should observe three key elements of the ceremony if the *Lila* is being performed genuinely. If any of these distinctives are absent, then the *Lila* is not being performed legitimately, and may be just for show.

1. First, the event will be overseen by a *cheikh* or *ma'llem*, who will be assisted by a small cult (*taifa*) of initiates.

2. Second, the ceremony will involve the sacrifice of a live animal, most usually a goat or ram, less frequently a cow or camel if the ritual is sponsored by a wealthy client or *zaouia*. The color of the animal is relevant, and indicates which class of spirit is being invoked. The concept of 'self sacrifice' does not exist in mainstream Aissaoua tradition, and the self-mutilation which takes place during extreme trances is **not** considered part of the sacrifice practices.

3. Third, the ceremony will involve music and singing. The Aissaoua believe that the spirits are drawn to song, rather than to prose speech. The majority of an Aissaoua ceremony is chanted or sung, not spoken.

Distinctives of the Azzeddini

The *zaouias* which follow Cheikh Azzeddine employ the same practices for the performance of the *Lila*. Even on a close examination, there is no evident difference in terms of the ceremony, preparations, sacrifices, or music. The primary difference then is in the range of spirits which are considered permissible in terms of trafficking. In other words, the mainstream Aissaoua will invoke local *djinn* which are known to be benign – or if not clearly benevolent, at least open to negotiation. The mainstream Aissaoua will not deal with the Shaitan (Satan) or the *shayatin* (lesser devils), as these are understood to be entirely malicious and without any redeeming characteristics which would make them worth the risk of entering into a relationship of any kind. The Azzeddini, however, have a fundamentally different view of the state of angels and devils, and of the ruling powers of the universe, as noted in the cosmology outlined earlier.

Following his epiphany at *Kaf el-Jnoun*, Cheikh Azzeddine has taught an emanationist cosmology, which puts the *Haawiya* (the 'Absolute' or 'Abyss') as the origin of all beings and states of existence, including non-existence. Cheikh Azzeddine considers the spirit or awareness of the Absolute to be the Quranic equivalent of the *Taghut* or the *Shaitan*. The Quranic deity, Allah, is considered to be a demiurgic subcreator, responsible for shaping the universe out of the Absolute, rather than ex-nihilo. The angels, *djinn*, and humanity are likewise shaped by Allah, though their substance is of the universe, and thus 'stolen' from the Absolute. Recognizing that Allah is an usurper, two legions of angels rebelled against his usurpation and seek to return the universe to the Absolute – the chieftains of these two legions are the angels Iblis and Azazel, both of which are classed as *shayatin* (devils) thereafter in the Quranic and hadith corpus. The *djinns*, like humanity, are of several groups, some of which are for Allah, some for the Shaitan, and some (perhaps most) are ambivalent or heedless of this struggle.

Since the Azzeddini follow this particular cosmological model, their spiritual exercises consider the *shayatin* to be noble and righteous spirits, albeit dangerous and inimical to most of humanity. The *Lila*s performed at the Azzeddini *zaouias* frequently begin the rites with prayers and invocations to Azazel and less frequently to Iblis as well. This practice is one of the easiest ways to distinguish the Azzeddini sect from the mainstream, as even the wildest Aissaoua *zaouias* will usually not invoke Iblis or Azazel as patrons, though they may be referenced by other *djinns* during states of possession. The Aissaoua-Azzeddini do not see these spirits as evil. They see *all* spirits as potentially dangerous, but that is not the same thing as seeing them as innately malicious. This likely comes from the strong African influences on the Aissaoua tradition, because most traditional African religions do not have a concept of 'evil' spirits. Spirits are viewed to be like people: they can be kind, or cruel, and sometimes even a very cruel person can be very nice if they are approached the right way and spoken to in a very humble manner.

Like the mainstream Aisssaoua, the Azzeddini believe that interaction with spirits is necessary for spiritual growth and development. As the spirits invoked tend to be from the more aggressive *shayatin* (rather than the *djinn*), the possession ceremonies tend to involve more aggression than would be expected in a *Lila*

THE BLACK PATH

involving the elemental spirits invoked by the more mainstream branches of the Aissaoua fraternity.

Another significant distinction from the mainstream Aisssaoua is that the Azzeddini do shed their own blood as part of the sacrificial practices. This does not replace the animal sacrifices, which are entirely obligatory if the spirits are to be properly invoked. But the Azzeddini initiates will make a demonstration of shedding a small portion of their own blood, which is often mixed with ceremonial wine, and offered as an oblation to the spirits. This may be combined with the self-mutilation practices which are carried out while in *ecstase*.

CHAPTER TWO: INSTRUCTIONS

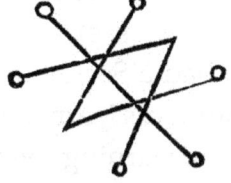

The Secret of Secrets

(Cheikh Azzeddine was asked about the *Sirr ul Asrar* (Secret of Secrets). He answered as follows.)

The essence of the esoteric path (*tariqa*) is the Secret (*Sirr*). The Secret cannot be bought or sold or written down, it can only be transmitted from the heart (*qalb*) of the *cheikh* to the disciple. It is that simple. The *cheikh* in turn receives the Secret from his *cheikh*, who received it from his *cheikh*, and so on. Every prophet and every saint has a Secret. Sidi Musa (Moses) had a Secret, and Sidi Suleiman (Solomon) had a Secret, and Sidi Aissa (Jesus) had a Secret. Their students learned the Secret from their prophet, just as you are learning the secret from me.

Science has many answers about the world, but the answers keep changing. Scientists used to say that humans could never fly, but now we have airplanes. They used to say that time is constant, but Einstein says that time and space are relative. They used to say that we came from giants (Adam and Eve), but now Darwin says that we come from monkeys and lizards. So science, you can't trust it entirely. You don't reject it, but you don't trust that it is going to be the same science tomorrow. But the Secret is not like that. The Secret is real, genuine knowledge. It is called 'a secret' for several reasons. First, most people do not know it, and they don't have the ability to understand it. Next, even if a very wise person tried to communicate the secret to someone who was not prepared for it (through a genuine *cheikh*), that someone would likely not understand it, or they might mock it, or insult it, or abuse it in some way. The Secret is known to only a few people, and it cannot be understood by many people. It is a precious, very precious thing. It is like a magic diamond that only very special people can see. Even if I hold out this magical diamond to someone, unless they are able to see it, it doesn't do them any good. I am offering them this diamond, but they can't see it, so they will think I am playing a game. And a *cheikh* does not play games, because he does not have time for games.

The Secret is like the flame of a lantern. Imagine that we are all trapped in a large dark cave. Now, I am your *cheikh*, so I have a lantern with a bright flame. You, the *murids* (disciples), you have lanterns. Your lanterns are all a little different, and it is my job to help you prepare the lantern to receive the flame. I help you to polish the lantern and to clean the glass. I help you to clean the wick and make sure that it is not dirty, or too long, or too short. I help you to select the nicest, cleanest oil to put in your lamp. Then when your lantern is ready, I give you the flame. Some people take good care of their lantern, and the flame burns very bright. Some people have a harder time taking care of the lantern, and so maybe the flame will flicker about. But the flame of the lantern is the same flame that I had in my own lamp, and my own lantern does not get weaker because I share the flame with you.

Instead, the more lamps that get lit, the brighter and brighter the cave will become.

Now, I will give you the best instructions I can possibly give, but I need to be careful to whom I give the flame. What would happen if I gave the flame to someone who is reckless or stupid? That person might get careless and drop his lamp. The glass will shatter and the oil will catch fire, and he will get badly burned, and people around him might get burned too. Or what happens if I give the lamp to someone who is too intellectual, and doesn't act on my instructions? If I tell that person things like 'clean the glass', 'trim the wick', 'purify the oil', and instead he decides to go research glass, or read about wicks, but he doesn't DO those things, what will happen? His lantern will not burn well, and he will blame me for being a bad teacher. Or worse, what happens if he tries to experiment with the lantern while it is burning? He will likely break it and burn his hands badly, and then he will tell people how stupid and dangerous it is to have a lantern.

So I have to be cautious. This flame is a dangerous thing. It can either give light to the lantern holder, or it can catch fire and burn the person who misuses the lantern. The person holding the lantern is responsible, but the *cheikh* is also responsible.

The Secret is eternal and unchanging. It doesn't get greater or less because I am sharing it with you. But when you learn enough to properly care for the lantern, then you can teach someone else how to care for their own lantern. Once I see that you are good at giving instructions, then I will give you permission to share the flame. Of course, you need to be humble and acknowledge where the flame came from originally, do you see? You cannot say 'Oh, I made this fire myself, I hit two rocks together.' That would be a lie, and your lantern would shatter and you would get burned. People do get burned, because the flame is alive, it's a living thing and it has a consciousness. You need to be honest and say where you got the flame from, and I am honest with you, I have told you where my flame comes from.

You asked me: what is the Secret? The Secret is a spiritual fire. It is a little like a spirit, though it is not really a spirit, but it has some of the characteristics of a possession spirit (*djinn*). When you join the *tariqa*, the *cheikh* will give you a small spark of the flame. He will tell you the exercises that are needed to increase that spark into a raging inferno. Once you get the spark, you don't need more fire. In fact, even if your *cheikh* tried to give you a big piece of fire, it will not matter if you have not prepared a suitable lantern. So the prayers, the invocations, the fasting, the *Lilas*, they are all to help you modify and improve your lantern so that one day it becomes a lighthouse, a tower with a great bonfire at the top.

Many people, they go to the *cheikh*, and they say 'Oh, my life would be so much better if you would just make me into a lighthouse.' But they don't understand that the *cheikh* cannot make them into anything. Only a person can improve their own condition. The *cheikh* can tell them how to become a lighthouse, but he can't do the work himself. It's true, a real *cheikh* will be able to help them. He can't do it for them, but he can assist. He can hire a foreman to oversee the work (this is the *zaouia mokademme*). He can hire additional laborers to help with the construction (these are the *djinn*). If he sees that there are rocks or trees in the way, or if there is a bad person who keeps trying to snuff out the fire, the *cheikh* will ask the village strongman to take a big stick and beat the thief, maybe even kill them if they persist in the thieving (this refers to calling on Azazel or Iblis to deal with enemies). Sometimes a person says 'Oh, I want to build my lighthouse, but I am too busy with my wife or my parents.' Well, he better be careful! The *cheikh* might report this to the strongman, and there are consequences (this is a warning about not putting family ahead of the *tariqa*). Or sometimes a person might ask me to help them build a lighthouse, and then I find out that they are building a lighthouse with another architect. Then I will dismiss the student, or maybe have the laborers rough him up a little for wasting my time. And even if I was soft and did not mind people playing naughty games, the flame itself is not a tame creature. Even if I was feeling indulgent and wanted to give the flame to someone who made all these mistakes, I would run into problems. The flame in my own lamp might decide to burn me, or to singe my fingers just a little. Even a *cheikh* can get careless, and the flame will burn anyone who does not treat it with the proper respect.

Look, what I'm offering you is not just a Secret. Other prophets and saints have Secrets. I am offering you the

Secret of Secrets (*Sirr ul Asrar*). If you go and study with the saints from the other Sufi families, they will turn you into a servant of Noor (the Light, a title of Allah). But Noor (Allah) is not the real light, it is the false light. Noor is a bad spirit that brings hatred, and bitterness, and warfare. Its light is darkness. You can see what is happening in Algeria right now, it is the work of Noor. Noor gives its secrets to the other *cheikh*s, and those secrets are real. But they are not good secrets, they are just secrets. I have been given *Sirr ul Asrar*, the Great Secret. I do not just want to help you get a good house or a good job or a good marriage – not because these things are bad, but because the Great Battle is coming. I want to prepare you for the end days. And we can prepare, because we have the Great Secret. So I will share the Great Secret with you, because I was ordered to do so by my own master. And my master is not Cheikh Ben Aissa, though he was the teacher of my teacher. But rather, my master and your master is Azazel, and He has given me the Secret on Kaf el-Jnoun so that I might give it to you. And I am working on you, and beating you up sometimes, so that your lantern is worthy of the fire that He has given us to wield.

Fire cannot touch something without changing it. It destroys what is weak and feeble, and demonstrates what is strong and pure. When a meteor falls from the sky, thrown by the angels, it is burning, burning, burning. The stone and chaff burns away, and the iron is all that remains. The Secret is the flame. When you join me, I give you the Secret. I put it in you, like putting a flame into a lantern made of precious glass, stuffed with oily rags. You try to clean yourselves, but you cannot get rid of the oil stains. But the fire will burn and burn inside of the lantern. It will consume the oily rags and the oil marks, and leave the lantern bright and shining for all to see. You are like a precious gem, covered in dirty thatch and straw. The fire will burn away the thatch and straw, and then the gem will be revealed for all to see.

If you think that you can get the Secret and not get burned, you are fooling yourself. Once you get the Secret, it will burn you inside and outside. If you have made preparations to receive the Secret and if you obey me, you will not get burned too badly. It will be a good burning that removes the bad only. But if someone does not take the Secret seriously, they will be burned badly, losing the good and bad in equal measure. That type of person will be reduced to a shell, they will not be good for anything.

Allah says in the Quran: 'Surely We brought man into being out of dry ringing clay which was wrought from black mud, and the *djinn* We created before from scorching fire' (15:26-27).

Do you see? Do you *see*?

Allah makes humans out of black mud and the *djinn* from the fire. But the Secret is able to reverse even this! When I give you the Secret, your spirit begins to burn in you, you become like the *djinn*. And the *djinn*, they get to become mud and clay through their interactions with you. Fire becomes clay. Clay becomes fire. This is the work of the Secret.

If you tell someone, 'Look, I will turn clay into fire,' they will laugh at you and call you crazy. If you also say 'Hey, this fire will become flesh and clay', then they will also laugh at you. You cannot tell them the Secret, but you will know it is true, because you will feel the fire burning in you.

    The Secret is power. I am not speaking in fancy riddles, I am speaking to you simply just as I would speak to a friend. The Secret is a small part of the *Haawiya* (Absolute) which exists in this world, just as this world is really inside the *Haawiya*. Allah says in the Quran: 'Their mother is the Absolute. And what can make you know what that is? It is a dark fire, intensely hot' (101:9-11). This means that once you acquire the Secret, the *Haawiya* (Absolute) becomes your mother. It will care for you and protect you, and help you to grow. The Secret will speak to you, showing you visions. When you dream at night, it will be there, whispering to you. It will give you strength and courage. If you become fire, how will you be afraid of *Jahannam* (the Islamic hell)? You will not be afraid at all, because the real fire of the *Haawiya* will already be a part of you, and you will have become a part of it while you are still alive. It is a living thing, it is like a spirit that possesses you and wants to become all of you, in time. This is what I have been trying to tell you. What is the Secret? It is the breath of the Shaitan. He breathed out of the Absolute into Azazel, and Azazel breathed it into me. The Secret is working to change us, so that we will be like them. You are not ready to enter the Black City, but the Secret is making you ready. It is eating you alive from the inside, devouring the man so that you can become the *wahsh* (beast). The Shaitan does not leave the Absolute, but through the Secret, He is with us and in us.

There is another aspect of the Secret. I told you before, each *cheikh* and prophet has their own Secret, and my Secret is greater, it is the Secret of Secrets. When your *cheikh* gives you his Secret, he is making you a part of his family. We have the Qadiri family and the Tijani family and the family of Cheikh ben Aissa (the Aissaoua). I have given you my Secret, which means you have become my children. And I have been given the Secret from our master Azazel, who has gotten it from his great father, the Shaitan. So we are like the children of the Shaitan, and this brings a great responsibility. The Secret is the heartblood of the parent. If we have accepted the heartblood of a monster, what does that make us? It makes us monsters too, at least a little bit. So when you accept the Secret from a *cheikh*, you can't give it back, it becomes part of you. It is not like taking on and off a shirt, it is more like going to the hospital to get a blood transfusion. Even if you get angry with me and you leave me in anger later, you can never get away from me, because it is my Secret that is inside you. And I can never leave you, I am always with you by virtue of the Secret, and my master is with you and me too.

THE BLACK PATH

Cherish the Secret. It is the greatest lesson I can give you. It is really the only gift I can give you that will do you any permanent good. If I give you money or expensive clothes, you will spend them and soil them. Eventually, material possessions will rot and fall away. But the Secret will grow inside you, slowly, until you are bright and burning and changed to be eternal like our mother is. And that is the only real lesson worth learning, because no other gift is of any value after we reach the grave.

THE BLACK PATH

The Need for *Bay'ah* (Initiation)

(Cheikh Azzeddine was asked about the role of Bay'ah (initiation, allegiance). He answered as follows.)

Education is simple. You find a teacher, and you check that he or she is a good teacher. You ask people, 'Hey, what is this *ma'llem* like? What is this *cheikh* like? What have you heard?' If you want to learn to be a hunter, then you find a teacher who is known to be a good hunter, maybe a great hunter, who knows about animals and tracking and making traps and snares. If you want to learn to fish, you find a good fisherman, someone who knows where the fish are, and what kind of fish are good to eat, and what kind of bait you should get to catch the biggest fish. If you want to be a physician, you find a great healer who knows herbs and medicines and poisons.

Now, if you want to be a hunter, you must not go to a physician. Some fool might say, 'Oh, this physician is so learned! He has so many books! Inchallah, I will go study with him and he can teach me more than the hunter because he has so many books.' And if the physician is unwise, he might even try to teach the fool. But even the greatest physician cannot teach you to be a great hunter, it's very clear and simple.

I'm telling you this because some people think that *ruhaniyya* (esotericism) is something that you can learn from books and classrooms. Some Sufis thought this, like

Ghazali, thinking that they could write books about the Secret, or explain it in books, or tell people about divine things on paper. But that doesn't make any sense at all, if you do not practice it.

Look, let us say that there is a poet. He is a very good poet, and he is excellent with words. He knows different languages, and all the rules of poetry. He knows the different genres, the meters, the alliteration and rhyme. He is a great poet. And now, he wants to write a poem about love. Well, if he has been in love, and knows the pangs of love, then it is ok. But what if he has never been in love? Then he cannot write a poem about it. 'Oh wait!' says someone, 'but he is a great poet and knows all about poetry!' Well, that may be true, but what good is his poetry if he doesn't know the subject? In order to write a poem about love, he will have to fall in love, and experience love in its sweetness and its bitterness. After three or four pretty girls have broken his heart, or after he romances a girl and gets married, then he is ready to speak about love. And even then, the reverse can happen too. There are many people who want to write poems about love, and they know all about love! Oh, they have gotten married many times, or they have been great lovers, and had many men or many women fighting for their affection. But what if they have not learned about poetry? If this is the case, then even though they might have some knowledge of the subject, they cannot teach others about it. They can have a real experience of it, but they are not good at sharing it or communicating it to other people, no matter how expert they are at love itself.

THE BLACK PATH

Let me say it differently to make sure you understand. A person can be a genuine adept at their craft, but not be a *ma'llem* (teacher). We see it in artisans – there are many good leatherworkers and stoneworkers, but they are not necessarily the best teachers. When parents want to apprentice their boy or girl, they need to quietly ask around to see if the leatherworker is an expert craftsman, or if he is also a *ma'llem* (teacher) of the craft.

It can happen that a student studies with a person who genuinely knows the trade, but cannot teach it to someone else, because they have no patience, or maybe they have a bad temper and will hit the student. That will only frustrate the student and make them run away from the subject.

Having said that, the true master of the craft must be a teacher. To become a master, you have to teach. It's the rule for all the trades – if you want to be recognized at the highest level, you must take an apprentice and turn them into a tradesman. Why is this? It's to show that your knowledge is real, and that you have such a level that you are able to make other people into skilled tradesmen like yourself. You cannot be everywhere all the time, but if you have three or four good students, then it's as if you are in three or four places, because it's your knowledge that is doing the craft, even though it's through someone else's hands. The same holds true for spiritual crafts as well.

So what about Sufism? Ah, Sufism. Well, it is like hunting. We are hunting for the spirits. Our master is Azazel, and he is teaching you to hunt. He has given us precious instructions (the Secret) and set our feet on the right path (the Black Path) that leads to our prey. Our master loves you, and so he sent me to be your guide. I am telling you now and every day, 'Hey, follow me, I can show you where the prey is!' But how do you know that you can trust me? Maybe I am a good guide, maybe I am a bad guide. First, you ask other hunters: is this Azzeddine fellow any good? Does he know how to hunt? Does he know how to teach people to hunt? Then you meet me, you ask to see my tools, and you ask about how I was trained. This part is important – you need to make sure that I had a good teacher. My teacher was the best, I was taught by Azazel. He still teaches me, he is my *cheikh*. So you check my credentials, and you make a decision once you are sure of my ability to teach you.

You are asking me about the bay'ah. Well bay'ah is hard to explain in French (the language of these talks). When you come to me and you say, 'Please teach me to be a hunter.' Well, I am not sure how serious you are, and maybe I don't know if you are already studying with another teacher. So I don't accept you right away, unless I know your family or your parents. But you are really insistent, you have a lot of determination to become a great hunter. So you ask again and again, you refuse to leave until I agree to be your teacher. Eventually, to show me that you are really serious, you make an oath, and I have to accept it. It's like swearing fealty to a prince – you take my hand, and you swear that you will obey me in all things, if I will accept you as my student. If I accept, then from that day forward, you have to do everything I ask you to do, in order to make you the best hunter I possible. If I say jump, you jump. If I say run, you run. You see?

Sufism is like this. If you really want to learn *ruhaniyya* from a *cheikh*, then you need to swear obedience to the *cheikh*. This is because the *cheikh* is not just teaching you a simple trade, he is teaching your very soul. He is giving you pure knowledge and trying to change you into a new creature. In our tradition, I want to help you to become something that can go back into the *Haawiya* (Absolute). My task is to make you a fit vessel for the Shaitan. The Shaitan cannot use you or enter you if you are not prepared. You need to be prepared. So my task is to toughen you up, and get you ready so that He can use you correctly. Of course, many of the tasks are not easy, and they are not all pleasant. Some of the things I ask you to do may seem hard or even crazy. I might tell you 'get married' or 'get divorced' or 'hit that fellow over there', or even 'drink poison', do you see? And when I tell you to do these things, you must do them. If you obey me, then you will earn my *baraka* (blessing), but if you don't, then I can't help you and the *baraka* will leave you and go somewhere else.

So this is why you need bay'ah. You cannot teach yourself, and the bay'ah is your connection to your teacher, and your guarantee of the quality of teaching that you will receive from him or her. The bay'ah is your chain, it is your invisible link to the *cheikh*, and through him, to his *cheikh*, and his *cheikh*, and so on. Without the bay'ah, you can still learn from a teacher, but he or she will not be your teacher, they are just a person who is giving you information. But the bay'ah makes that particular *cheikh* into your own personal spiritual guide and travelling companion on the road. So whatever path you decide to walk, whether it is the Black Path, or some other path, see to it that you find a guide and make a firm commitment to them.

Now, not all people have easy access to a guide. There are many people in Europe, even in America, who are sensitive to the truth, but they cannot find a spiritual guide. Most of the *cheikh*s are here in Africa, and most of them are teaching half-truths, because they have been taught half-truths by their *cheikh*s. So what can we expect of these people? They cannot help the situation. No, if someone learns about the Secret, and about the *tariqa*, and they have a deep desire for spiritual truth and to receive the blessings of the *Haawiya*, then they need to get a *cheikh*, there is no confusion here. There is a noble saying in Arabic: 'He that has no teacher, his teacher is the Devil.' Normally people think that this is a bad thing, but in our tradition, it becomes a good thing. When someone needs a *cheikh*, but there is no *cheikh* to be found, *Sidi'na* (Our master) Azazel will become the *cheikh* for that person. If someone wants to make real progress upon the Black Path, then they should pray to Azazel to appear to them in a dream or vision, so that He can give them the bay'ah directly. Then He will give them the

Secret, and then they have the means to begin on the path. Of course, that person will have a very hard time – do not think otherwise! And this is not an excuse to avoid finding a teacher. But if there is really no way to find a *cheikh* or *ma'llem*, then our master Azazel will act as the *cheikh*, until the disciple is able to find his human *cheikh* later on. But to take Azazel as the *cheikh*, the *murid* must have a genuine intention to obey Him in all things. In many ways, this is very difficult, because Azazel is not a person, and so He will give instructions to the person that may be really superhuman. But He is closer to the *Haawiya* than you or me, so He is able to give very strong *baraka* to His students. I am speaking from experience here, because Sidi Azazel is my teacher, and He has tortured me cruelly to make me into a good *cheikh* for you. He makes me suffer daily, but my suffering is good, because I am suffering for your sake. A good teacher makes mistakes, so that his or her students do not make those same mistakes.

THE BLACK PATH

The Role of the *Tariqa* (Esoteric Lodge)

(Cheikh Azzeddine was asked about the role of *tariqa* (esoteric lodge). He answered as follows.)

We are at war. You are a soldier on the battlefield, fighting a war that you were thrown into. You didn't choose to be a soldier, and I didn't choose to be a soldier either. But we are born into a spiritual war, and there are spiritual enemies all around us. They control the government, and our culture, and they control the religions too. You can see the damage of the war playing out all around us: people dying over water, people dying to get more oil, people killing each other to maintain a filthy rich habit of life. The rich religious people are the worst: look at the Saudis! Monsters, they are bloated and swollen on the Quran. They treat women like donkeys, they rape their domestic servants, and they treat Arabs from the West even worse than they treat the Americans. Where is the Islam? Where are the Christians? Well, they are the real villains. The Pope calls 'peace, peace, peace', but the Vatican is invested in drugs and weapons. As long as people are following Allah, there will be only blood and warfare, and He will keep them fighting and fighting because as long as they are fighting each other, they will not fight Him. Most people are asleep, they don't know that they are in a spiritual war until it is too late. They die trapped in a religion of the Book, and then Allah will seize their soul and probably put them into his jail. Allah made the humans and jinn, but He secretly hates them because their essence is stolen from the *Haawiya*, just as His essence is from the *Haawiya*. He is ashamed that He is just a sub-creator, not a creator (*huwa b'hal khaliq, lakin huwa mishi khaaliq*).

So you have woken up, and you realize that you are on the battlefield. What choices do you have? You can try to run and hide, but Allah will certainly catch you and put you in chains. Before they were not concerned with you, because you could not see them. But now that you can see Allah's angels, they will not spare you. So you cannot run. Well, you have two choices. You can join the enemy, and become a religious person. You can be a Muslim or a Hindu or a Jew, it doesn't matter, because Allah controls them all. If you are a good little Muslim or good little Christian, He will even reward you. Yes, it's true – if you follow Allah, He can protect you from His own attacks, and shelter you. You will be a traitor against your own people, and you will always know that you are a coward, but you will be safe, at least for a little while.

You have another choice: you can join the spiritual resistance army. You can find a battalion that will take you in, shelter you, feed you and protect you, and they will teach you how to fight. They will put you in boot camp, and teach you to act like a real solider. Then you will not be a victim anymore. You will be dangerous, a real monster. If the angels try to come for you, you will fight them off, or even take them captive. So what is the rebel army battalion? It is the *tariqa*. The *tariqa* is your army battalion. The Shaitan is our great general. He commands the entire army, and He wants you to become a hero, a champion (*batal*). So He has sent Azazel and Iblis to form battalions. Sidi Azazel is our colonel, and He has formed the Assiaoua battalion, but He is busy with other units too. So he made me the commandant in charge of the battalion. *Wailiii* ('damn it!'), it's a lot of work. But I am fortunate, because the *wahsh* (beast) helps me to train you. The *wahsh* is your drill instructor, it is always watching you, always ready to punish you if you do not do your best. The *wahsh* is merciless, and it wants to turn you into a *wahsh*. Inchallah it will succeed.

So the *tariqa* is your battalion. When you join, you belong to a *taifa* (cell). Maybe your *taifa* has a base (*zaouia*), maybe it doesn't. The important thing is that you're not fighting alone, you have comrades. Now, when you join, there are other veterans in your unit. You don't know any of the tricks of the trade, but your comrades know all the tricks. So they help you out. Instead of letting you make some bad mistakes, they tell you, 'Hey, the commandant does it this way, so we do it this way too,' or 'Hey, don't do that, the commandant won't like it!'

Sometimes you get tired and you think, 'Oh, I will rest a little now, and inchallah it will be no problem.' But your *taifa* sees that you are tired, and they encourage you, they cajole you a little. Maybe you have exercises that you should be doing, but you're tired and don't want to do the exercises. On your own, you would quit and go home, but you know that your comrades are watching you, and you don't want to let them down. It works the other way too: you might be new to the team, and when the comrades see new blood joining, they are encouraged. They don't want to slack off in front of the new blood, so they redouble their own efforts, so that you are impressed by the level of their performance.

You might wonder why I used the metaphor of a military unit. And my answer is this: it's not a metaphor. We really are at war, there is an actual spiritual struggle going on in the universe. I think people are actually aware of it deep down inside, because we're torn in two directions if we're honest. Part of us wants to serve Allah (under whatever name), and to grovel like dogs and beg for His mercy. But part of us knows that feeling is the kind of feeling that kidnap victims get for their captors – it's not a real love, it's a sick kind of love that a slave has for its master. Deep down inside, we want to sin and rebel and do things independently, and we don't want to be told what to do. We feel cut off and depressed, because we used to be part of the harmony of the *Haawiya*, but we were taken away by force. But the good news is that we are not victims, we have agency (*qadir*) and we can fight back. The Shaitan has not abandoned us, and instead He has sent His best champions to teach us how to fight. So we must train, we must really work hard and we can become the terrible and awe-inspiring heroes that the Shaitan wants us to be. If we succeed, we will be immortal. If we fail, then at least we will have another chance to get it right.

THE BLACK PATH

You must choose your side. Choose to be the predator or the prey. Then once you have chosen, find your army and get to work training to be the kind of spirit warrior that can make a difference in your own life, and in the lives of those around you.

THE BLACK PATH

The Nature of the *Wahsh* (Beast)

(Cheikh Azzeddine was asked about the nature of the *wahsh* (beast). He answered as follows.)

To understand the *wahsh*, you need to understand how Adam and Hawa (Eve) were created. We have said earlier that Allah is the Light, and He calls himself the Light in his book of half-truths. He says, 'Allah is the Light of the heavens and the earth' (Quran 24:35). But he cannot create something from nothing, and even he does not make this enormous claim. Instead, he steals the raw materials from the *Haawiya* and gives it shape. He is a craftsman. Look, how does he make our father and mother? He says, 'We created man from sounding clay, from mud molded into shape' (Quran 15:26). So he takes the clay, and shapes it into a human. Then he breathes into the model and it becomes alive, because his own spirit animates it. But his spirit is not his own, because Allah emerged from the *Haawiya*, and someday he and his cosmos will be forced to return to it, because he and it do not exist independently from the Absolute.

There is the *Wahsh Kbeir* (Great Beast) and the *Wahsh Sgheir* (Lesser Beast). I will tell you about the Lesser Beast first.

A man has three parts: *jesed* (body), *ruh* (soul), the *wahsh* (beast). This beast is the *wahsh sgheir* (lesser beast). The

Arabs also call it the ego (*nafs*), but we do not really use this term in the Black Path. We understand the body, because it is how we touch and feel and experience the world around us. It is solid, flesh and bone. The soul, we cannot touch it, but it is the seat of our intellect and thinking powers, it is also the cord that connects the man to Heaven. The soul is the seat of *mantiq* (logic) and critical thinking, and it is the source of the false ego. The *ruh* tries to trick you and make you think that you are 'it', and not 'you' or the body. But the *wahsh*, we don't understand it well, and the religions try to suppress it and beat it down. The *wahsh* is the source of our emotions. It is the source of instincts. The *wahsh* is the mediator between the body and the soul. It is the seat of all pleasures, as well as wrath, lust, and pride. Of course, it is necessary for the survival of the human being, you cannot remove it or else you are just a corpse. A body on its own is clay, and a soul on its own is just a ghost, but the *wahsh* is the personality. It is instinct. You know when you meet someone who looks nice and speaks nicely, but you know instinctively that they are a bad person? That is the *wahsh* talking to you. Or when you work with someone, and they are always smiling at you, but you know that they really hate you? That is the *wahsh* which cannot be deceived. Or when you are speaking to a close friend, and they are telling you a story, and you suddenly know that they are lying? That too is the *wahsh*. It is the seat of our animal, and it is the source of intuition and hidden wisdom.

THE BLACK PATH

The *wahsh* is not entirely physical, and it is not entirely spirit. It is something strange, something in between. Some have said that it is the connection between the flesh and the spirit, a kind of medium between the physical realm (*dunya*) and the otherworld (*akhira*). When the Western doctors talk about the ego, this is the seat of the ego. Think of it – are you your body or your soul? You are really neither one, you are something in between. That is the *wahsh*, the animal spirit. When people go to war or they go hunting, and they experience feelings of bloodlust and rage, that is not the flesh or the soul, that is the *wahsh*, raging to be unleashed.

Why is the *wahsh* angry? It is angry because it knows that we have been born into a kind of slavery in this awful world. It knows that there is a spiritual war going on around it, and it wants to find shelter, and then to thrive. It senses that we are not meant to be as we are – we are neither animals nor angels, we are somewhere horribly in between the two worlds. The *wahsh* is the part of us that straddles the two worlds, and it is really a monster. It has to be a monster, because it is unnatural to exist in both worlds. The *wahsh* is also a vestige of the chaos of the Absolute – it is a reflection of the first beings that are in the Absolute. The first ones are monstrous, they are nothing even remotely human. We remember this, but not with our flesh or our souls, but rather with the *wahsh* which is our demonic nature.

No one knows for sure how we come to possess this inner monster. Some Muslims scholars have said that when the fetus is in the womb of the mother, Shaitan comes and puts the *wahsh* inside with His own hand. Personally, this is my opinion. Prophet Isa (Jesus) was the only prophet to escape the gift of the *wahsh*, and he was not able to get married, have children, or even preach beyond two years. No survival instincts! He had no *wahsh* to warn him about treachery, and so he was killed. Prophet Muhammad had a very strong connection to his *wahsh*, which is why Islam is so violent, and makes no apologies for this violence. My own thinking is that when Allah tried to fuse a divine soul into a physical body, He unleashed a part of the raw chaos and savagery of the Absolute. That is why people disobeyed him from the beginning, do you see? He made Adam and Eve and gave them simple instructions, but they disobeyed Him immediately. Then when they tried to have children, one brother killed the other. Do you see? That is the *wahsh*, raging against this unnatural state, against this separation from the Absolute. The *djinn* do not have it, angels do not have it, beasts do not have it, but we have it. We have it.

Now, many of the old Sufi masters wanted to beat down the *wahsh* to strengthen the soul, but that is stupidity. That is only useful if you plan to live in the *bled* (country) in a *zaouia*, and you never want to get married or deal with people. The Christian monks, they are very good at killing the *wahsh*. The *wahsh* wants to live, it wants to be free and to rut and to kill. You don't need to eat meat to live, the doctors say – but you like to eat meat. Why is this? It is the *wahsh* – it is a predator, and it compels us to kill and consume lesser beings. The Black Path is not a path of denying the *wahsh*, or trying to beat it down. The Black Path wants to release it, and to let it run free. Even the Aissaoua understand this much, which is why the *Lilas* have people letting their *wahsh* free, so that they are driven to bark like dogs, or howl like wolves, or roar like lions. That is the *wahsh*, raging in some way. It is not a peaceful animal, it is always an angry predator of some kind. In the Black Path, we are seeking ultimately to reach the Black City, and then to go through it to reach the Absolute. But how do we find the Black City and the Absolute? The *wahsh* knows the way. It senses the Absolute, and it knows how to get back. But if the soul is not chastened and weakened, then it will be a chain on the *wahsh*. So while we are here, we need to do practices that will allow the *wahsh* to consume the soul, so that it becomes a greater being. Otherwise, the soul may consume the *wahsh*, and then we become like Christian monks and nuns.

You ask me about the Great Beast. We know that in the end days, the Shaitan will send a messiah to guide us. He will unite the chosen ones, and he will oppress and persecute the infidels who follow the god of Abraham. He will punish the People of the Book, and will do signs and wonders. He will be the son of the Shaitan. Even the Muslims are expecting this – they talk about the Beast of the Earth (*dabbat al-ard*) in connection with the *Dajjal* Messiah. This is a metaphor, meaning that the *Dajjal* Messiah will arise from a man. That is, the Beast will emerge from the Man. It is double speak, do you see? So you and I and the other students of the Black Path, we are learning to release the Beast from the clay, so that we become the beast. But the Great Beast, he will be different, he will be better than you and I. He will be the living embodiment of the *wahsh* in human form, which has not been seen before. They say that the Dark Messiah will have only one eye, which means that his vision will not be divided. They say that he will come riding on an enormous donkey, and this is the symbol of the Americans, so he will perhaps be an American. They say that he might have the head of the boar, and this means that he will be very fierce and wrathful, because of his Father's furious wrath. When he comes, he will ask people to accept his mark, which is the mark of the Absolute. They say that he will have the staff of Moses and the Ring of Suleiman, and this means that he will have the power and authority over this world (like Moses) and the spirit world (like Solomon). His coming will herald the last great battle here, when the Shaitan will come forth with His forces, and Allah will come with His angels, and all creation on this planet will be divided. And we do not know what that day will bring, but we know that we must prepare. So the Dark Messiah is our master and commander, and he is also a symbol of what we are trying to become.

So how do we do this? You need to learn to listen to the *wahsh*. It speaks to you, did you know this? The Quran tells people to take refuge with God from the voice that whispers inside (*waswas*). But on the Black Path, we say that this whispering voice is the only voice that you can really trust, because it is the only voice that speaks wisdom. I give you advice, and your family gives you advice, and your imam gives you advice. But who knows best? The *wahsh*. The *wahsh* cannot be fooled, because you cannot fool the Absolute. The *wahsh* is your connection to the *Haawiya*, whispering to you, telling you how to get home. Sometimes the whispers are very unpleasant, because they do not lie. We lie to ourselves all the time, because we are not honest with ourselves. We lie to our friends also, to spare their feelings. But the *wahsh* does not lie, it does not know how to lie very well. It is direct, and yet it is not logical. The *wahsh* does not give you advice based on logic, because logic is a chain of Allah. There is no logic or reason in the *Haawiya*, because logic is a handicap. And humans are not very logical, not if we are being honest. We can use logic, but that does not make us logical. We are creatures of passion and instinct, which comes from our true nature.

So when you need to make a choice or decision, or you are at a crossroads, concentrate on your inner voice. Silence your mind, silence the intellect. Listen for the voice in your heart, in your stomach, in your blood. Blood makes noise, so listen for that noise. Do not always use logic – allow the *wahsh* to speak to you. It will scare you, because it is not human itself. It does not want to be human, and it does not want YOU to be human. But you must learn to listen to it. If you learn to listen to it, you will learn to become it. You must listen to it, and learn to obey it. Obey it, because it is the voice of our Father. If you learn to obey it now, it will protect you when you die and acknowledge you before the Father. But if you deny it, then it will deny you in the grave, and deny you before the Father.

Look, you say that I am your guide, but I cannot really guide you. The *wahsh* inside you, it is the only real guide, because it comes from the *Haawiya*. I can give you advice and teach you some practices that I have from my own *cheikh*, but I cannot be with you all day. But you do not need me, your real teacher is inside you. I do not mean this the way that most Sufis do, when they say that Allah is in the heart. They are partially right – Allah is within the *ruh*. But you need to put the *ruh* to death, and in doing so, the *wahsh* will be free to advise you. I tell you the truth: on the day that you have put your soul to death, you will be able to speak to the *wahsh* the way that you speak to your closest friend. The *wahsh* does not want to leave you – it wants to be you, to be all of you. And when you die, it is the *wahsh* that will survive you, if you follow my teachings. Because if your consciousness is seated in the *ruh* when you die, you will go to Allah's Hell. But if you have put the *ruh* to death, and your consciousness is seated in the *wahsh*, then you cannot ever really die. The *wahsh* is eternal because it is an extension of the *Haawiya*. So put the soul to death. I tell you, put the soul to death.

The Nature of the Shaitan (ﷺ)

(Cheikh Azzeddine was asked about the nature of Shaitan. He answered as follows.)

The Shaitan is very difficult to explain in human words. If you really wish to know the Shaitan, you must first learn to commune with your *wahsh*, and then it will explain the Shaitan to you. As the Secret grows within you, you will understand the Shaitan better and better. But since you have asked, I will tell you what I can tell you.

In the beginning, there was the *Haawiya* (Absolute). It was all darkness and chaos, and it was filled with the primordials (*bida'ioun*). These first beings were great monstrous things, they were really very complex emanations of the *Haawiya* itself. The *Haawiya* is very difficult to explain, because it is entirely outside of our universe. The Quran says that Allah is *rabb al-alaameen* (lord of the universes), but the *Haawiya* is outside of all the universes, and they are inside of it. The first beings, primordials, they were all connected, like trees sharing roots. The first among them was the primordial known as *Al- Taghut* ('the Alien'), and it was sometimes called *Taneen* ('Dragon') in old stories. It has no real name because the primordials do not have names as we do. It has an emanation in the cosmos, which we call the

Shaitan or Azazel. In Arabic, Shaitan means 'he that is outside, he that is far away', and that is because the Shaitan is from outside of this universe, He is not originally a cosmic being (*huwa michi min l-koun, wa huwa michi kouni*). The other first beings, they are related to it, but *Al-Taghut* is their sovereign. When we say that it is a dragon, we do not mean a lizard that breathes fire, but a great terrible beast with no equal. When I say 'dragon', you think of a great monster, and that is the closest explaination that I can give with words. Arabic is a very simple language, it does not have many words for monsters.

The Light appeared, and declared itself to be Allah ('the deity'), the only God. The Quran says, 'Allah, there is no deity save He' (2:255), but this is a hollow boast. So Allah made his seven angels, and they made war in the Absolute, thinking that they would overcome the dragon and its monstrous kin. This story is familiar, no? It is the same story that the first peoples told, in Babylon, in Egypt, in Greece. It is in the Christian book too. The Jews speak of it, they call the Dragon 'Leviathan'. There is eternal enmity between the Dragon and Allah, and that struggle continues in this world and in all worlds. For now, the struggle is invisible, and many there are who deny that it is real. But it is real, and the prophecies of the Great Battle are unfolding. The Great Battle is coming, and when it comes, we say that Allah will be punished. He will be devoured by the Dragon, and the universe will perish in blood and water. All will collapse, star by star, back into the Absolute. This is an old story, and it is told in many books. Why do all these people have this story? It is because we remember it. Then, we were part of the *Haawiya*, and so we were silent witnesses. This story is in our blood and bones, and it becomes part of all our great tales. When Allah tore us away from the mire of the *Haawiya* to shape the universe, the scars of that struggle came with us. The making of this comsos was a trauma (adhi) and a trial (fitna). We cannot forget it, even though we cannot remember our conception or our birth or even our childhood.

In the Absolute, there are other beings, and they are mighty and terrible. They do not forget the struggle, and they have not abandoned us. They do not love us, for love is not part of their nature. But we are their kin, drawn from the same substance of which they have a greater share. The *wahsh* is the passive link to them, and the Secret is the active link. They desire our return to the *Haawiya*, and they do not accept that we and the cosmos should exist in rebellion against the *Haawiya*. The *Haawiya* is our mother and their mother, and they will not accept that a universe exists outside the *Haawiya*. Of course, there are many worlds and universes in the *Haawiya*, but this one is an abomination, because it is outside the *Haawiya*. In the *Haawiya*, all beings enjoy unending bliss and perfect knowledge, but Allah is selfish, and so He created this universe. In the *Haawiya*, all things are connected, and nothing exists separately – there is no clear division between us and the Shaitan and the *Haawiya*, because things do not exist or not-exist, it is very different from this world. But we know that in this world, we are separate, and so we are suffering. We need to get married and to have children and friends so that we are not alone, because we are flawed.

The Shaitan does not want us to be flawed. He does not want us to exist at all, unless we exist together through Him. And so He gives us the Secret through our Master Azazel, and he gives it to me, and I give it to you. The Secret is busy, busy reintegrating within us. It is dissolving you slowly from the inside, rebuilding you so that you are not a person, you are a part of the Shaitain. That is why Islam says that some people are devils. This does not mean that low scum are devils – they are just pigs and dogs. No, a devil is someone who has overcome themselves, they have sacrificed their humanity to become something more. The soul needs to be destroyed for the integration to take place, so Shaitan gives us *dhikr* (meditation) and *salah* (prayer) and *ecstase* (trance, ecstasy) to make us forget the ego. The *ruh* (soul) gives us false ideas of culture and society, and tries to make us 'behave'. It is like a bad police officer in your head, threatening you with a baton whenever you start thinking thoughts against your culture. And what is our culture? It is a trap, a mental sickness that focuses us on Allah. Look, see the world today. The Muslim hates the Jew, the Jew hates the Muslim, the Christian hates them both. All three faiths are focused on Allah, but they are busy trying to kill each other. Why is this? It is the *ruh*, it is Allah's little trickster, forcing people to kill each other and fight each other and hate each other. Allah wants to be separate from the *Haawiya*, and He wants to keep us separate. If we are separate, we feel alone and weak and threatened, and we are forced to rely on Him. Do you see? Is this not a great sin, a great outrage?

The Shaitan is like a great intelligence – it is almost wrong to see Him as a single being, He is a collective spirit. When Prophet Jesus spoke to the possessed man, what did the demon say? 'We are legion, we are many' – well, that means that this spirit was very close to the *Haawiya*, because it did not think of itself as a discriminate entity, it thought of itself as part of a collective. The Shaitan is also a separate mind, but He is a mind in touch with all the minds of the *Haawiya*. His is not the only great mind, as the other great first beings are also very powerful. They are very alien from us, and very hard to speak to, and they are almost closer to forces of nature than to individual beings like us. It is like being a private in a large army, and having to try to talk to a general – what would you say? What would you have in common? So it is like this, they are the generals, and we are the privates. Now, they do speak to us in dreams, and they can enter this universe when they wish to, or send their shadow into this world. Many magicians like Suleiman, they think that they can summon Azazel, or Belial or Zaganiyya, but they cannot do this. All they can do is maybe get the attention of the great devils, and perhaps the great devil will send a fraction of its essence to deal with the magician. It is not the same as trying to summon the *djinn* – you can learn to call the *djinn*, that is easier. It is dangerous, true, but they can be called, and spoken with. The *djinn* are closer to the *Haawiya* than we are, but they are closer to us in nature than the primordials. But when a sorceror or Sufi claims that he will call the Shaitan, then he is a deluded fool.

Sometimes, the *djinn* can enter into a *murid* or medium (*shwafa*). This can be painful at times, if the *murid* is not experienced and tries to fight the *djinn*. The *djinn* can stay inside for years at a time, though the greater *djinn* will not do so, because the human body is constrictive for them. The greater beings in the *Haawiya*, they cannot enter into a *murid* at all, because they are too immense. Instead, at times they will overshadow a human, so that their power (*baraka*) flows through the *murid*. This is the experience of the prophets and saints. The mortal flesh is clay, and it cannot hold spirits of fire. We must walk upon the Black Path, so that we are changed to be like the Shaitan. This is not a poetic expression, it is a real truth. I am speaking simply to you, not using philosophy. The *Haawiya* is our destination, and we must become changed to reach it.

The Shaitan wants to affect the world, and it pleases Him sometimes to affect the world through us. You must realize that He does not need to work through us, but He chooses to do so, and so do the other great primordials whenever they choose to do so. If we are not aligned with His will, then we are of little use to Him. But He is not the murderous and joyless creature that sent the Prophets – He does not launch crusades between his own worshippers. The Shaitan does not tempt people to wickedness or sin, as such concepts do not exist in the *Haawiya*. Rather, the confusion between the flesh and the soul is responsible for the awful deeds, and this is further complicated by the cold commandments that are given by Allah in his awful books. Do you see how Allah hates women? He claims not to have a mother, or a wife, and no children. He denies women the right to equality, and begrudges them even the few rights that they have. The Shaitan does not care about gender, and all the primordials are beyond gender – though we perceive some as 'male' (muthakr) or 'female' (mu'anath). That is not to say that they are asexual, as the *Haawiya* is filled with continued mixing and seeding between the great monsters that are there, but that their gender is not fixed so firmly as it is in us. But Allah hates and fears females like Lala Zaganniya (Allat) or Lala Uzzat (Al-Uzza), who are our grandmother. Lala Uzzat is the feminine manifestation of the fertility of the *Haawiya*, and Lala Zaganniya is the mother of all the fiends in the *Haawiya*, and we are Her children. If we forget Her, then we become the prey of Her children. This why some mystics and saints still pray to her, though they call her *Aicha Kandicha* in some places, and *Eisheth Qadesha* in others. And Allah hates Her because He is male and not female, and He did not create female angels even.

The Shaitan and the primordials, they want us to return to them. They are jealous and angry that Allah has shattered the unity. So He will be punished – we do not know how – but until that day comes, we must remain faithful to the Shaitan, for He is our father and will not forsake us.

THE BLACK PATH

CHAPTER THREE: PRACTICES

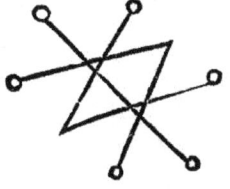

Overview

This chapter discloses the practices of the Aissaoua tradition, as adapted by Cheikh Azzeddine. Most prominent are the fundamental practices of *dhikr* (divine mindfulness) and *wird* (spiritual litanies), immediate practices such as trance and sacrifice, and advanced practices like possession, esoteric intercourse, and skin-changing. The Aissaoua tradition is not meant normally to be an individual tradition, and there is great emphasis on the *taifa* (cell) or *zaouia* as a working community.

THE BLACK PATH

THE *ZAOUIA*

The Sufi can practice anywhere, but it is very helpful to create a space that is private and suitable for intense spiritual practices. We call this space the *zaouia*. The Aissaoua tradition, including the Azzeddini, is very simple. You do not need a fancy house or building, you just need a quiet room. In fact, *zaouia* means corner in Arabic, so even if you do not have an entire room, you need just a corner of a room that you can dedicate to your spiritual practices. In Algeria, Morocco, Tunisia, it is normal to have a dedicated room in a house, or in areas with a larger Sufi population, a dedicated building. So you need to decide whether you can manage a corner, a room, or a building.

A *zaouia* does not need to be greatly decorated. This is one advantage that comes from the Arab spiritual traditions: sacred space is recognizable by its lack of objects, so it is called a negative-space tradition. In our own specific branch of Aissaoua, we hold that we show respect to the *Haawiya* by a general lack of physical objects. Still, it is good to have a number of things to help create a positive spiritual atmosphere. The following items may be useful to acquire:

- RUGS: It is good to be close to the ground for practices, so we keep rugs or carpets on the floor.

- INCENSE: It is good to have incense to make the air fragrant, and this is necessary to attract certain spirits.

- MUSIC: sacred music is a major part of the Azzeddini tradition. While there are certain types of music that are native to North Africa, Cheikh Azzeddine insists that every region has its own music which is appropriate. What is important is that the music have a strong beat, in order to help inducing trance states.

- SACRIFICIAL TOOLS: blood sacrifice is another major part of Aissaoua practice. Traditionally, a good sharp knife is necessary, and this should be kept aside wrapped in black cloth when not being used in the ceremonies. It may be also advantageous to have buckets and water to help with the butchery of the animal in question. It is assumed that the meat will be consumed (cooked or not) by the participants.

- TASBIH: traditional practices often make use of prayer beads – these can be knots tied into a cord, or bone or stone or wooden beads threaded onto a string. Normally, the *tasbih* has 99 or 100 beads.

- TALISMANS: the Aissaoua tradition favors the creation of talismans, which are objects that contain the *baraka* of the *djinn* or angels. These are used normally for protection, but can be used as curse objects or to carry a specific *baraka* power.

Consecration and Resonance

There is no clear concept of ritual consecration of places or spaces in the Aissaoua confraternity. A place or an object becomes holy or profane by the practices that are carried out there on a regular basis. Cheikh Azzeddine is fond of saying that on the final day of their construction, what is the difference between a bar and a mosque? Absolutely none – and they will often have the same customers too! There is no ritual, no ceremony that can make a *zaouia* into a *zaouia*. A *zaouia* becomes a *zaouia* through use. Even if we build a dedicated *zaouia* structure, but we neglect to use it, at best it will become a hostel for *ghuls* and other dangerous spirits. The same principle applies to a mosque: if no one prays there, then it is not really a mosque, it is just a big empty building that looks nice.

That said, the Aissaoua do believe that spiritual resonance can be created. We know this more from criminal places than holy places. When a terrible crime is committed somewhere, a particular resonance or vibration is formed there. It's not a question of good or evil or anything like that, it's more a fact of the natural laws of the esoteric world. Consider this: if we go to the ocean and find a nice beach, can we swim safely? Probably yes. Now, if someone takes a bucket of fresh blood and begins to dump it into the water, can we still swim safely? Of course not, because the blood will attract sharks and worse things. What is this? It's resonance.

The same principle applies to holy structures: through the practices, the prayers, the rites, the place develops a certain resonance. But if you go to an abattoir, it's an entirely different resonance, and you don't need to be a spiritual person to see this, it's just a question of moderate awareness.

So we apply the same principles to a *zaouia*. Now, can we create a resonance that is conducive to the particular *djinn* or spirits that we wish to attract? Yes, of course. With the *djinn*, resonance is a question of color and scent and taste. The *djinn* are part of this world, and so when we wish to interact with them, we need to create the proper resonance that will attract them, or repel them if there are spirits we wish to discourage. Take the *djinns* of the seas and oceans – these tend to be gentle spirits, and are attracted to water and the color blue. If the *zaouia* is intended to host these kinds of spirits – and it might, if the *zaouia* is right on the coast – then you will decorate the *zaouia* typically with carpets and rugs that are deep blue in color, and you will have bowls of scented water in the *zaouia*, in case the spirits are thirsty. If someone is hoping to attract the *djinn* who are attached to the court of *Sultan el Aswad* (the black sultan), then you can guess already that there will be black colors, black candles, and strong incense. This is resonance. As a perversity, Allah uses resonance too in His book. What does Quran say that the Muslims will find in Heaven? Beautiful virgins and good food! See, even Allah is trying to coax you into His world, because maybe you would not want to go if you could see it for the static tomb that it really is. So we should not be ashamed to use resonance, because it is used by us, and it is used on us too. All this is to say that you should build your *zaouia*, assuming that it will become a *zaouia* through long-term use, but you should furnish it according to the types of spirits that you hope to have in residence there frequently.

THE BLACK PATH
UDHIYA (SACRIFICE)

Cheikh Azzeddine is fond of saying 'blood makes noise.' That is because shed blood, especially in ritual, is very loud in the esoteric world. The Quran and the Torah are not wrong when they say that 'the blood is the life.' Blood spilled in this world, especially when it is offered to the spirits, attracts them like it would a great predator in the water. If we are serious about our spiritual practice, and we are really serious about creating an environment that is conducive to the proper spiritual states of mind, as well as to the beings that we want to welcome, then blood sacrifice (*udhiya*) is necessary. Many modern spiritual groups have abandoned practices involving blood, but African traditions continue to emphasize blood rites, because they are extremely effective.

When selecting an animal for sacrifice, it is necessary to identify the preferences of the being to which the sacrifice is being offered. Is the sacrifice for the Absolute? Then it can be any living being, and in primitive times, this included human sacrifices. Is it for one of the *mala'ika* (angels)? Then a bull or camel is customary. Is it for a *djinn*? In this case, it depends on the particular *djinn*, but usually some manner of sheep or goat, or even poultry is acceptable.

For *murids* and clients who live in Africa and the Middle East, blood sacrifices are a practice already common within Islam, so no special precautions need be stated. For those living outside these regions, it should be stressed that sacrifice is by cutting the throat of the animal. The animal is not meant to suffer, and the stroke should be swift and clean. The blood must be collected, and this is used as a separate offering in a lengthy rite where multiple spirits must be 'fed'.

It is also tradition that the animal be cooked afterwards, and the meat of the sacrificial animal is held to contain much *baraka*, especially if it has been offered to the Absolute or its angels.

THE BLACK PATH
DHIKR (REMEMBRANCE)

Dhikr means 'to remember', and it is not easy to translate out of Arabic. To understand *dhikr*, you need to understand that in Arabic, the human being is called *al-insan*. *Insan* has as its root '*nsn*', which means 'to forget'. So humans in Arabic are the forgetful ones. We forget all kinds of things. We forget to do things we intend to do. We forget a birthday or a celebration. We forget to tell our friends that they are important to us. We forget the pain of an injury or a betrayal. Even a death of a relative, we forget how it makes us feel over time. We are forgetful. Worst, we forget where we come from. We are really in bad trouble – most people have no idea of their spiritual origins, or the origins of the universe. The Quran says 'Allah made it all,' so we say, 'Oh how nice, Allah did all this, so we owe everything to him.' And He even makes fun of humans in some prophetic sayings, it's like Allah points at Adam and says 'Oh, you stupid forgetful human! Of course, I made you to be forgetful, but you must apologize for being forgetful all the same!' What a desperate and insecure deity He is. So Islam says that Allah makes us forgetful of our origins. In fact, Muslim tradition says that Allah had all the souls of all the humans in Paradise before He created the earth, and He forced them to acknowledge Him as Lord. Then He cursed the humans (us!) and took away their memories, and caused us to be born in flesh, without the memory of

Paradise or Him, and all this life is a grueling test to see which humans will somehow crawl back to them.

So the Shaitan, because He is wrathful at Allah's deception and trickery, He calls on us to remember. Not to remember the groceries or our grudges or our pains, but to remember that we are not mortal. We are eternal beings, cut from the *Haawiya*, torn from our dark mother, and we do not belong in this universe. This universe is an abomination. Of course, we have nothing against a physical or material world – our traditions says that there are hundreds of physical and material worlds, and when we return to the Absolute we shall be able to enter into those worlds and enjoy all sorts of pleasures without limit. We shall hunt and eat and kill and breed without reservation or limit. But this universe is an abomination, because Allah created it outside of the fullness of the *Haawiya*. So it will be destroyed and reintegrated. But for the moment, the Shaitan calls on us to remember who and what we are. We are not mortals, we are immortal spirits trapped in a body. The soul is the chain that forces us to forget, it is really a curse. But the *wahsh* remembers, and we need to make sure that our waking mind, the thinking mind, it remembers also. If we can remember and stay remembering, then it will be very hard for Allah and His angels to trick us and trap us, even in very chaotic circumstances.

Dhikr, remembering, it has two modes. One is the active mode of *dhikr*, and the other is the passive mode. In general, we need both, it is no good to cultivate one and not the other. I will explain.

- **Active *Dhikr***

We need to start with active *dhikr*, which is the *dhikr* of beginning, and the *dhikr* of establishing a pattern. When we decide that we want to become mindful, which is to possess *taqwa* (mindfulness), we must take time every day to focus our mind on remembering. In other spiritual traditions, this is called meditation. It is good to perform active *dhikr* within our *zaouia*, in whatever form the *zaouia* takes.

Active *Dhikr* is a very simple practice: the *cheikh* or *ma'llem* or *mokaddeme* assigns a specific phrase, always in Arabic, which must be repeated a certain number of times. Usually the *cheikh* will specify if the phrase should be said 100 times, or 500 times, or 1000 times, etc. Some phrases are good for beginners, others are more complex and are not revealed until a solid foundation is established. It is also good to mention that while silent *dhikr* is permissible, audible *dhikr* is much preferred in the Aissaoua tradition.

The purpose of active *dhikr* is not to overthink the phrases or the state of emotion it provokes. *Dhikr* is not an exercise in logic, it is an exercise in instinct. By repeating the phrase, we hope to awaken the *wahsh* and to incite it to connect fiercely with the *Haawiya*, and then to empower us in turn. To say it differently, by performing *dhikr*, we are feeding the *wahsh*, and allowing it to grow stronger from the spiritual essences that we invoke through the *dhikr* practice.

The following phrases are authorized by Cheikh Azzeddine for new members of the *tariqa*. We refer to these as the *Asma el Haawal* (Terrible Names):

- **Ya Shaitan** — Oh Satan
- **Ya Mul Wahhoush** — Oh Master of the Beasts
- **Ya Sultan el-Aswad** — Oh Black Sultan
- **Ya Ataghut** — Oh Absolute
- **Ya Haawiya** — Oh Absolute
- **Ya Lala Zaganiya** — Oh Lady Zaganiya
- **Ya Lala Uzzat** — Oh Lady Uzzat
- **Ya Lala Aicha** — Oh Lady Aicha

Instructions:

1. Sit comfortably in a chair, or seated on the ground.

2. Choose one of the *dhikr* phrases to recite.

3. Take the *tasbih* (rosary) and 'thumb' one bead along the cord.

4. Intone the phrase in Arabic, as you move the bead.

5. Do not *think* about the phrase. Rather, *feel* the phrase.

6. Repeat until you have finished the entire tasbih, then repeat until you have recited the mandated number of tasbih rounds.

The idea is to perform this particular practice, confident that you are attracting the attention of the spiritual power to which you are addressing yourself. Believe with conviction that even if you do not feel any immediate connection, eventually the eyes of our masters will turn in your direction. It can takes hours or days or even weeks, but you will eventually feel the strange sensation of being watched. It is critical that when you sense even the slightest presence, you accept it as a genuine occurrence of *baraka*. Even if you feel perhaps that you are imagining it, it is important to accept it as a real phenomenon. The powers in the Absolute will reward you for your devotion and increase your ability to perceive them. Of course, it is not that you are trying to get their attention, but rather that you are trying to attune yourself so that your *wahsh* can hear Their voices, which otherwise are drowned out in the spiritual 'radio static' that the universe drowns in.

There are some traditions that teach that *dhikr* can be done silently, or that it is even best done silently. Our master, Cheikh Azzeddine, does not recommend *dhikr* to be silent, and this is for several reasons. First, silent *dhikr* is easily distracted. A person who is chanting internally may find that their mind wanders and the chanting stops.

By vocalizing the chant, you are better able to focus the mind.

Second, *dhikr* is a supernatural act, and the very name of the entity being spoken aloud is the same as the deity. The Shaitan lives in its name, so to speak, so to say 'Shaitan' out loud is to experience the being. This is the reason why pious Muslims will not say Shaitan out loud after dark, because of the very real possibility of attracting His attention. But this is for us an encouragement – if a Muslim is afraid to chant the name of Shaitan even once for fear of attracting His terrible eye, then what of the Azzeddini who chants Shaitan or Layla hundreds and thousands of times? Do you see?

Third, to chant the name of the Shaitan or the other devils is to experience them physically. Sound is vibration, and vibration courses through the living organism. By chanting the black names (*asma saouda*) out loud, you are uniting your flesh and spirit in the adoration of the entities to which they are connected. The verbal component is necessary for your flesh to engage in the worship process. Chanting the *asma saouda* is equivalent to incarnating them, even if it is only very briefly. This is very important, as the great beings in the Absolute are excluded from this world by Allah, so by deliberately invoking them, you are creating a doorway for them and bringing them into this world. This changes you permanently. You cannot chant *dhikr* longterm without creating passive *dhikr* effects, which I will discuss below.

There is also what is sometimes called 'lesser *dhikr*', which is *dhikr* of the *djinn*. Often, the Aissaoua tradition works with the local spirits. These *djinn* and *djinna* are closer to Shaitan than we are, and they are easier for us to interact with. They are in a sense our intermediaries. You cannot ask Shaitan to help you get a job, maybe, but you can ask Sultan Al Aswad. You cannot ask Mother Lilith to give you sex, but you can ask Lala Aicha for sex, and she will fuck you. Oh, she will fuck you to death maybe! (Azzeddine laughs here.) Do you see? So sometimes a *murid* will ask the *cheikh* permission to do lesser *dhikr*, and then the *cheikh* will give the *murid* practices that will help create resonance with the particular *djinn* that the *murid* hopes to attract.

- **Passive *Dhikr***

Now, there is another kind of *dhikr*, this is passive *dhikr*. It is easy to explain. Let us say that someone wishes to attract Baba Hammu, for some dark business, like to cause revenge or death. Now, the first thing to do is to ask: what do we know about Baba Hammu? Well, first, he is the patron of the abattoirs. This is because he is a terrible *ghul* who drinks blood. He loves blood, and he loves violence. There are even stories about children who play outside at night, against their parents' wishes, and they are suddenly seized by an unseen force and carried screaming into the darkness. That is Baba Hammu. Baba Hammu loves red, and sharp blades, and blood. So a client comes to the *cheikh*, and says that they want to kill an enemy. The *cheikh* says 'yes, very good'. So now what? The client needs to create the conditions to get Baba Hammu's attention. The *cheikh* will do a *Lila* (ceremony) of course with a sacrifice, but that is only part of the work. The client needs to do things to please the spirit. He needs to remember (*kidhikr*) the spirit, to be constantly thinking about him and obsessing about him, in order to draw the spirit's attention. Do you think it is easy to attract the spirits? It is not. No, it is not. So the client needs to find a way to be constantly in a state of *dhikr*.

To make this possible, the client will first wear the *djinn*'s color. In this case the *djinn* is Baba Hammu, so the client will wear red. That way, whenever the client looks in a mirror, they see the red and remember Baba Hammu. Next, if the *djinn* likes a particular scent, the client will wear it. Most *djinn* like perfume of some kind, but Baba Hammu likes blood, so it's harder in this case – the client has to cut themselves and rub a small bit of blood on their neck and wrists. Not much, just a little. And all this time, the person is constantly thinking 'Come, Baba Hammu! Come Baba Hammu!'

This is an extreme example. Let me give another example. If a *murid* is really devoted to Ummna *Haawiya* (Mother Absolute), they will wear black. They will wear black kohl on the eyes, and black jewelry if possible. They will decorate their homes with black cloth and black paints. They will spend time outdoors in the evening, looking up to the darkness between the stars. Do you see? This is not because they want something, this is because that *murid* longs to return to the *Haawiya*. They don't want anything in this world. This is for people who are of a gentle disposition. They do this to create a constant ongoing resonance with the *Haawiya*.

The act of passive *dhikr* is also tied to active *dhikr*. Active *dhikr* becomes passive *dhikr* if we do it often enough. If you are really serious about becoming a living vessel for the *djinn* or the greater spirits, then you will need to do active *dhikr*, and if you do it often enough, then you cannot stop doing it. I know several serious *murids* and *murid*as, and they used to chant 'Shaitan, Shaitan, Shaitan' day. Now, they do not chant actively, because they cannot stop chanting. Shaitan is no longer an external force, He is a part of them. They have killed their own spirit through active *dhikr*, and through passive *dhikr* they have created the conditions through which the Shaitan has been able to enter them and establish His Throne within their hearts. That is the supreme triumph.

Of course, there are different ranks of accomplishment. Some people will always be a client, some people will become a *murid*, and a few people can become a *cheikh* or *cheikh*a. A client does not want to do any regular practices – they just want to benefit from the *tariqa*. There is nothing wrong with clients, on the contrary, we are happy to have them. When someone says 'look, I will sponsor a *Lila* in my home, for good luck', or someone says 'my daughter cannot get a husband, can I sponsor a *Lila*', that is all good. That is building the Black City here on earth. When people are recognizing the Aissaoua as a community that they want to be involved with, even if they don't enter it, it is good. Some people go beyond this, and they ask the *cheikh* to accept them as a student. They ask to be taught and guided into experiences. This is even better than a client, because this person is saying 'look, I want to go down to the Black City, I want to serve Father Shaitan and Mother *Haawiya*.' And that is really noble if they are sincere, and the *cheikh* will accept them and give them the Secret. A few *murids* will have the capacity for sainthood, they will become the forerunners of the *Dajjal*, helping to prepare His kingdom here on earth. These people have the Secret in great measure, and they desire to share it with others. They are called the *cheikh*s and teachers of this noble tradition.

The difference between the three ranks is the level of *dhikr*. The client does active *dhikr*, maybe. The *murid* does active *dhikr* and passive *dhikr*. And the *cheikh* has internalized *dhikr*, which is to say that all his *dhikr* is passive.

THE BLACK PATH
THE *WIRD* (LITANY)

The *wird* is the daily liturgy of the Azzeddini *tariqa*. It is considered an obligation that every *murid* recite the *wird* at least once a day, without exception. The *Wird* helps to connect the members through a common practice, and it creates a very powerful resonance. In a sense, the *wird* is the *tariqa* itself, they are inseparable. Anyone can do *dhikr*, even a client can receive a *dhikr* practice from the *cheikh*, but the *wird* is special. In previous centuries, the *wird* was protected, and still today maybe *tariqas* do not share the *wird* openly. In this century, Cheikh Azzeddine teaches that the *wird* should be made available to anyone who wishes to engage with the practice. As it has been said elsewhere: 'They who have no *cheikh*, their *cheikh* is Shaitan' – which means that sincere practice of the *wird* will result in the *Baraka* of the highest and best of spiritual masters. The *wird* also functions as a type of spiritual protection, and those who engage in the *wird* on a daily basis will begin to experience increased otherworldly presence, even during very mundane situations.

Anyone can begin to say *dhikr*, but to enter into the *baraka* of the *tariqa*, one needs to make a commitment to the *tariqa* and its *wird*. Of course, nothing prevents someone from just memorizing and reciting the *wird*, but they will simply receive a trickle of the spiritual power that is available for those who have made a genuine commitment. It is similar to saying to someone that you can try to swim in the pond or in the ocean – swimming is swimming, but the experience will not be the same between those two extremes.

The *wird* of the Azzeddini-Aissaoua is as follows:

- *Bismileh alathi arsala alayna malaika wa ruhu wa jnoun fi hada dar alazeem. Wa huwa ala kulu che'in qadir. (100 times)*

- *Subhan Azazel (1000 times)*

- *Ya Umna, Ya laila, ya latifa (100 times)*

- *Ya Taghut (100 times)*

- *Fa ummu'hum l-Haawiya (1000 times)*

- *Ilahumma, Sali ala sayiduna Azazel wa ala ahlihi wa sahbihi tasleeeman. (100 times)*

THE *ECSTASE*

One of the distinguishing features of the Aissaoua *tariqa* is *ecstase*: the wild, ecstatic trance states in which the society engages. While other Sufi orders place great importance on a calm, sober communion with Allah, the Aissaoua hold that the divine is chaotic in nature, and that contact with it does not lead to social order, but rather a kind of degeneration of behavior into primitive, atavistic states of consciousness. If a saint is truly in the grip of the Absolute, he or she will not care about proper etiquette or comportment, because they will be operating on completely inhuman frequencies. The Azzeddini go beyond this, as the founder teaches that the genuine touch of the Absolute is very empowering for the *Wahsh*, which is likely to seize control of the Aissaoua. The reports of the Aissaoua as a lycanthropic cult ('confrérie lycanthropique') is actually derived from outsiders witnessing rites that are meant to be private, wherein the *murids* work themselves into a trance through chant and drumming, and seek to allow their *wahsh* to run free. This appears similar to possession, except that there is absolutely no invitation of the *djinn* for possession – rather, the *murids* work to arouse their own inner passions and desires. In extreme cases, groups of *murids* will enter a violent *ecstase* and will attack those who are unfamiliar or wearing colors that are considered 'triggers' like black or red, which the Aissaoua themselves do not wear, except for *Lilas* involving possession.

Since it is very difficult (and potentially dangerous) to engage in *Lilas* independently, Cheikh Azzeddine has authorized *murids* in remote areas to instead focus on practices of *ecstase*.

The following are a set of simple instructions which can help to induce this particular spiritual state:

1. Secure a location which will be safe from interruption. Privacy and isolation are critical for the successful performance of this rite. The location should be dimly lit and incensed.

2. Invoke the benediction of the Cheikh and Sidi Azazel, then take refuge with the Absolute.

3. Recite with the Azzeddini *wird* in its entirety.

4. Play music with a powerful and steady beat, ideally without lyrics. Traditional African music may be suitable, but local music is equally suitable. (NB. Some *murids* in Paris report industrial rave music to be very effective.) The music is not as important as finding a beat that feels compelling.

5. The *murid* should rock back and forth in time with the beat.

6. Focus on a particular vice or desire. It can be lust, anger, pride, etc. Allow the mind to descend into a vivid mental enactment of the desire.

7. Allow the vice or emotion to become all consuming. Concentrate on the feeling of satiety, rather than the object of the visualization. For example, a *murid* might fantasize about a particular taboo sex act. They should vividly imagine the sex act, allowing the mind to explore every detail. Eventually, the image of the sex partner should be subsumed into the lust itself, and then the *murid* themselves becomes dissolved into the lust.

8. Visualize the vice or emotion itself dissolving into the *wahsh*. There is nothing left except the *wahsh* and its overwhelming hunger and power.

9. Hold the image of the self as the *wahsh*. Allow the *wahsh* to move through you. At this point, the *murid* may rage, scream, caper, and engage in any activity that does not cause serious harm to oneself, others, or the environment.

10. Visualize, when the rage subsides, the *wahsh* superimposed over the human flesh. Feel the *wahsh* surging through the mortal coil.

11. See, after the ego (*nafs*) has returned to normal consciousness, that the 'ego' is a false construct, while *wahsh* is the genuine personality.

12. Follow any future guidance or advice from the *wahsh*, which the *murid* should record and make pains to act on, if possible. Powerful new urges and instincts may arise, and these should be sated as often as possible.

THE BLACK PATH
THE *LILA*

The *Lila* is the central ceremony of the Aissaoua. It is a group practice, and requires the presence of a *mokademme* (master of ceremonies) and a chorus (*taifa*) of Aissaoui. The *Lila* is often performed at the request of a client, who will 'sponsor' the event in their own home, or at the *zaouia* if they cannot afford to host it at their own residence. The *Lila* is always a nocturnal event, and the name itself means 'night-time' (Arabic '*Lila*'). This is for two reasons: one, most of the *murids* and clients are understood to have professional commitments during the day, which would make their presence and participation difficult; second, the *djinn* and spirits themselves are shy of the daylight, and do not normally manifest during the daylight hours.

The purpose of the *Lila* is always determined in advance. If the *Lila* is sponsored by a client, it can be to secure the benediction and support of whichever spirits for very mundane reasons. It is normal to host a *Lila* to celebrate an event (a birth or wedding), or to ask the spirits to help in case of a family, professional, or medical crisis. If the *Lila* is hosted by the *zaouia* itself for its own members (and not clients), then the event can be for worship, or to establish and maintain good relations with the *djinn* patrons of that region.

THE BLACK PATH

The rite is very complex and has layers of traditional hospitality and procession, which are difficult to communicate in text. Cheikh Azzeddine suggests that for the sake of those potential *murids* who wish to establish a *zaouia* or *taifa* abroad, that the procession and pageantry can be largely omitted.

The rite proper has three core components which are:

1. *Dhikr* (The Remembrance): this practice has been described above in pp. 106, and refers to active *dhikr* as a group ceremony. The *murids* are already well versed, and the clients are invited to 'join in' as the *mokademme* leads the group through the liturgy. The *wird* of the Azzeddini is usually the basis for the group *dhikr*, though this can be dispensed with if time is short. This part of the ceremony is necessary, as it helps to create the correct spiritual resonance which will facilitate the second and third parts of the ceremony.

2. *El Mluk* (The Possessed): this part of the ceremony is the spiritual heart of the *Lila*, in which the particular *djinn* or angels are invoked. This séance is never random, and is determined well in advance by the *cheikh/mokademme/ma'llem*. Unlike other occult traditions, the *djinn* are not evoked into an external appearance or manifestation, rather they are invoked into *murids* or clients who wish to be possessed. This can lead to violent or wild behavior, for which reason a *Lila* is never attempted without the presence and supervision of a *mokademme*. Equally, a *Lila* can be performed to help 'treat' a person who is already possessed. In this case, the séance serves to discover the identity of the *djinn* and to identify the needs or demands of the intruding spirit. While in modern times it may be fashionable to invoke or evoke spirits independently, that is not an Aissaoua practice. The main reason for this is that if a lone *murid* attempts to call the spirits and succeeds (which is very easy), the spirits are likely to invade the nearest person – this case, the hapless *murid*! Cheikh Azzeddine himself is no stranger to possession, and states clearly that an isolated *murid* who becomes possessed may do harm to themselves, or to leave the *zaouia* and engage in destructive or violent behavior. With some spirits such as Baba Hammu or the Aghwal, this is all too likely. Alternately, a person might engage in behavior that is sexually taboo or provocative if under the influence of one of the female *djinna*, which is not physically destructive, but can cause considerable social chaos.

3. Hadra (The Encounter): the final part of the *Lila* ceremony, *Hadra* is where the *murids* focus on the Absolute. After having performed *dhikr* and experienced the presence of the *djinn*, now the ceremony focuses on transporting the minds and hearts of the participants on the spirit world itself. Through a rhythmic chanting established by the *mokademme*, the *murids* enter a trance state (*ecstase*), which is characterized by rocking backwards and forwards together. Participants experience a sensation of dissociation with their bodies, and at advanced stages will lose any sense of distinguishing self. In place of their own individual ego, they experience the overwhelming presence of the Absolute, which is beyond any description, and can only be described through the esoteric language of the Secret. *Hadra* can be witnessed by clients, and some rare few outsiders will actually experience it, though without the internal esoteric power of the Secret to help make sense of the Absolute, the sensations are said to be overwhelming and nightmarish.

Music

One of the most important parts of the Aissaoua tradition is the strong reliance on music. This is likely due to the fact that music soothes (or arouses) the savage beast, and over the centuries the Aissaoua have found that music serves as a powerful tool of communication with spiritual forces that do not respond to human language. Music is, in a sense, the language of the heart, and a wise *mokaddeme* learns very quickly what manner of language works with which spirits. Music is tied to culture, of which it is a kind of expression, and so the spirits of a particular region are likely to be roused or calmed by music familiar to that region. Cheikh Azzeddine insists on using Berber, Arab, and French music in *Lilas* in Algeria, but he is equally opposed to using those languages when *murids* in Indonesia or Malaysia want to deal with the local spirit courts there. It goes without saying that the cosmic spirits and angels are not tied to any one culture, and they are more likely to be drawn to the human emotions released during a good performance.

Dance

One of the most universal of spiritual tools is dance. The dance of the Aissaoua is very simple, and often is limited to a circle or line of *murids* who rock back and forth in unison. Even the clumsiest and least musical people are often able to accomplish this, but it should not be underestimated. When clients witness the Aissaoua rocking back and forth for three hours, the atmosphere becomes entirely otherworldly. Dance can also be more exotic and acrobatic, and *murids* who are under the spell of the *djinn* can perform very inspired dances. The dancing of the Aissaoua is almost always simple and repetitive, for two reasons. One, dance is meant to strip away the inhibitions of the clients and *murids,* and it helps them to commune with their own *wahsh*. Second, dance induces trance, which is very necessary for possession and *hadra*.

Offerings

General offerings are those offerings which are presented at the beginning of the evening, and again at the end. Traditional offerings in Algeria are milk and dates, and a

European or North American equivalent could be milk and cookies. The *cheikh* will confer his blessing on them, saying 'bismillah' or other benediction. Specific offerings are more complicated, as each of the *djinn* have their own required fabrics, colors, and sometimes specific substances which they insist on having. Finally, the Aissaoua rites always have blood sacrifice as part of the *Lila*. This is because orthodox Islam insists that the *djinn* are blood drinkers, and so blood must be offered to have the spirits attend as guests. Several of the spirits have particular colors which should be reflected in the choice of animal sacrifice, and the blood collected from the main sacrifice will be used to 'greet' the specific *djinn* as they appear.

The Structure of the *Lila*

For those initiates who are distant from an actual *zaouia*, Cheikh Azzeddine has authorized the performance of the *Lila*, according to the means of the *murids*. Ideally there will be a group of Aissaoua present who are proficient in the ritual and music, and so instructions will not be necessary. However, for those initiates who are operating a new lodge in Europe or North America, the following steps can be followed and adapted.

THE BLACK PATH

Preparation:

1. Identify the purpose of the *Lila* – what are the needs of the spiritual client or community?

2. Select which of the spirits is best invoked, according to the needs identified.

3. Prepare the general and specific offerings.

4. Prepare ceremonial banners/flags and clothes.

5. Obtain music which will be played during the *Lila*.

6. Have the Aissaoua sit in a circle on carpets or on the ground, and have the clients sit comfortably to the side.

The *Lila* Proper

1. Opening invocation by *Mokademme*.

2. *Dhikr* (*mokaddeme, murids*, clients)

3. General Sacrifice, offerings (*mokademme, murids*)

4. *Mluk* (*mokademme, murids*, client)

5. *Hadra* (*mokademme, murids*)

6. Closing invocation (*mokademme*)

7. Refreshments (*mokademme*, *murids*, clients)

THE BLACK PATH
THE DJINN

Orthodox Islam holds that Allah created the three worlds, and then created the three kinds: angels from light, the *djinn* from fire, and humans from clay. All three were endowed with levels of intelligence and power, in descending order. The three materials represent the innate quality and power of the three kindreds, so angels are considered the highest and purest of beings, *djinn* are nearly as potent, while humans are weaker and duller than either of the angels or *djinn*. Angels are said to inhabit the celestial world, the *djinn* are native to the spiritual (esoteric) side of the terrestrial, but can enter the celestial. Humans are native to the material (exoteric) terrestrial level, and can learn to enter the esoteric level of the material plain through spiritual practices.

The *Djinn* of the Aissaoua are traditionally divided into three great families or categories, but to the *murids* outside North Africa, these distinctions will not mean very much. On the following pages, the author attempts to describe several of the most prominent *djinn* who are considered patrons of the Aissaoua and the Azzeddini-Aissaoua.

Unlike other spiritual traditions, the Aissaoua hold that these entities are very real beings, which exist separately and independently from humans. Like humans, they have their own society, politics, agendas, and desires.

The *djinn* are fascinated by 'our' world, and seek to manipulate our world for their own inscrutable reasons. Whatever has been written in western books on goetic magic, the *djinn* cannot be summoned or commanded. In fact, it is highly unlikely that ANY spirit which is independent of the witch's imagination could be. Contemporary oral tradition in Algeria has many accounts of people who have tried to coerce the *djinn* or summon them for petty reasons. This typically leads to horrific consequences, including harmful possession, sickness, misfortune, and accidents. For such reasons, the *djinn* are treated by the Aissaoua as respected friends or patrons, and dealt with in the most courteous ways possible.

Zawaj b'djinni (Spirit Marriage)

In many African religious societies, it is believed that the spirit world and the human world can come together in marriage. Cheikh Azzeddine says that French folklore has similar beliefs, especially when they speak of humans being abducted into the otherworld of the *fée* (fairies), which sometimes resulted in embarrassing pregnancies or foundlings. In the Aissaoua tradition, a client or *murid* who wishes to obtain special spiritual powers or good luck will sometimes ask to take a *djinn* in marriage. Alternately, a client or *murid* might find themselves demanded in marriage by a *djinn* who is invoked at a *Lila*. In either case, it is best for the *mokademme* to assist in formulating the contract of the marriage. The *djinn* themselves are not monogamous, and so their demands are usually relatively simple. For example, they will often include a demand that their spouse shall reserve one or two nights a week for conjugal visits. This is not a symbolic request, as the *djinn* are deeply sexual beings, and so on those nights, the client can expect to be visited by their 'spouse', who will proceed to initiate intercourse. As the *djinn* tend to remain invisible, this can be a startling experience the first few times it occurs. Other *murids* experience the conjugal visits as vivid dreams. Also frequently, the *djinn* may insist on particular offerings in exchange for their 'love', which translates into material good fortune. A *murid* who makes weekly sacrifices of blood and sugar to Lala Malika will find their interpersonal conflicts are 'smoothed' over, and their social challenges are made mysteriously easy. A client who is married to Chamharouch will typically find that the misfortune of others becomes their own good fortune. A rival company might botch several contracts, and an enemy may sicken or even die. Less maliciously, Chamharouch may help his spouses to see opportunities that were not visible before, or (more colloquially) to discover buried treasure.

Marriage with the *djinn* is not without risks. Clients frequently enter into it, thinking that a *djinn*-marriage is a quick fix for a long term problem, but this is disastrous thinking. Unless the contract clearly states that the marriage is temporary (fixed term duration), then the *djinn* may expect a permanent connection. Unlike other occult societies that suggest that spirits can be banished or commanded, the Aissaoua understand that the *djinn* are very real and very powerful, and if they feel that the contract has been broken, they may take revenge – or worse, they might take the contract to the spirit lord of the region, in which case the offending client can expect catastrophic bad fortune. If a *murid* wishes to remove themselves from a relationship for whatever reason, or to reduce the demands that they have taken on, they should seek the advice of a *cheikh* or *ma'llem* on how to do so.

Djinn Families

The following pages provide details on several *djinn* from the traditional Algerian families. *Murids* outside of Africa will have to investigate the spiritual traditions of their own locales, as the indigenous spirits will have their own courts, patrons, and lore which give insights into which can be addressed, and which should not. Also, not all spirits are blood-drinkers, and the *murid* should investigate the lore of their own region to see what offerings are traditionally accepted by the spirits. Some spirits prefer ritual immolation of grains or alcohol, or else flesh, or more exotic gifts.

THE BLACK PATH
SIDI MUSA (Jilala family)

Sidi Musa (Master Moses) is the patron saint of the seas, especially the Mediterranean. He is dressed in blue and likes offerings of water, especially sea water if possible. Sidi Musa is also the patron of travel and of liminal spaces, like the seashore and the coast, but also of the doorways to the spirit world. For this reason, the Aissaoua call him to help open the way to the other *djinn*. Sidi Musa is like the Mediterranean – he is generally warm and of good temperament, but he can be angered and stormy if he is not shown appropriate respect.

THE BLACK PATH

A *Lila* will often begin with his invocation, not because he is the strongest of the *djinn*, but because he is one of the most mellow, and it is hoped that his presence will encourage the others to 'behave', or at least to be less malicious than their natures might otherwise encourage.

When calling Sidi Musa, it is best to have the blue flags present, and to have the offering table draped in blue. Bowls of sea water or other natural water should be present. The *mluk* (possessed *murid*) will likely expect to consume one or more of these.

The traditional chant to call him is as follows:

Mokademme: 'Ya Sidi! Ya Sidi Musa!' (x 2)

Mokademme: 'Ya, Bab dyel Sidi Musa!' (x 2)

Chorus: 'Sidi Musa, smah'lina!' (x 2)

Chorus: 'Smah'lina, Sidi Musa. Ya Allah!' (x 2)

(ENGLISH TRANSLATION)

Mokademme: 'Oh Sidi, O Sidi Musa!' (x 2)

Chorus: 'Forgive us, Sidi Musa. O Allah!' (x 2)

THE BLACK PATH

Mokademme: 'Oh, the doorway of Sidi Musa' (x 2)

Chorus: 'Forgive us, Sidi Musa!' (x 2)

THE BLACK PATH
BABA HAMMU (Jilala family)

Baba Hammu is the patron saint of abattoirs and places of slaughter. He is fond of the color red, and the offering table must be draped with red to please Him. He is also drawn to fresh spilled blood, and so it is necessary to offer this to Him – otherwise He may be angered and cause great harm to all present.

If Baba Hammu appears through possession, it is necessary that blood sacrifice be offered, if it has not been offered at the beginning of his chant. If this is not carried out, he will possess one of the people present, and will inflict them with a long term wasting sickness, where he drains the vitality of the victim. Cheikh Azzeddine holds that if it is not possible to slaughter an animal for Baba Hammu, it may be possible to offer some of the *murid*'s own blood. This is not advised as a frequent practice, as one does not want this particular spirit to develop a 'taste' for the blood of the *murids* involved in his cult.

The chant to attract Baba Hammu is as follows:

Mokaddeme: 'Sidi Hammu, smahli'na!' (x2)

Chorus: 'Ya Sidi, smahli'na!' (x2)

Mokaddeme: 'Sidi Azazel, smahli'na!' (x2)

Chorus: 'Ya Mala'ik, smahli'na.' (x2)

Mokaddeme: 'Sidi Hammu, mul dar ad'dam.' (x2)

Chorus: 'Sidi Hammu, mul dar ad'dam.' (x2)

Mokaddeme: 'Bou tarbouch ahmar.' (x2)

Chorus: 'Bou tabouch ahmar.' (x2)

Mokaddeme: 'Aghwal bghaou shrub ad'dam' (x2)

Chorus: 'Aghwal bghaou shrub ad'dam' (x2)

(ENGLISH TRANSLATION)

Mokademme: 'Sidi Hammu, bless us' (x2)

Chorus: 'Oh Saint, bless us' (x2)

Mokademme: 'Sidi Azazel, forgive us' (x2)

Chorus: 'Oh Angel, forgive us' (x2)

Mokademme: 'Sidi Hammu, patron of abattoirs.' (x2)

Chorus: 'Sidi Hammu, patron of abattoirs.' (x2)

Mokademme: 'You who wear a red turban.' (x2)

Chorus: 'You who wear a red turban.' (x2)

Mokademme: 'The demons wish to drink the blood.' (x2)

Chorus: 'The demons wish to drink the blood.' (x2)

THE BLACK PATH
CHAMHAROUCH (Jilala family)

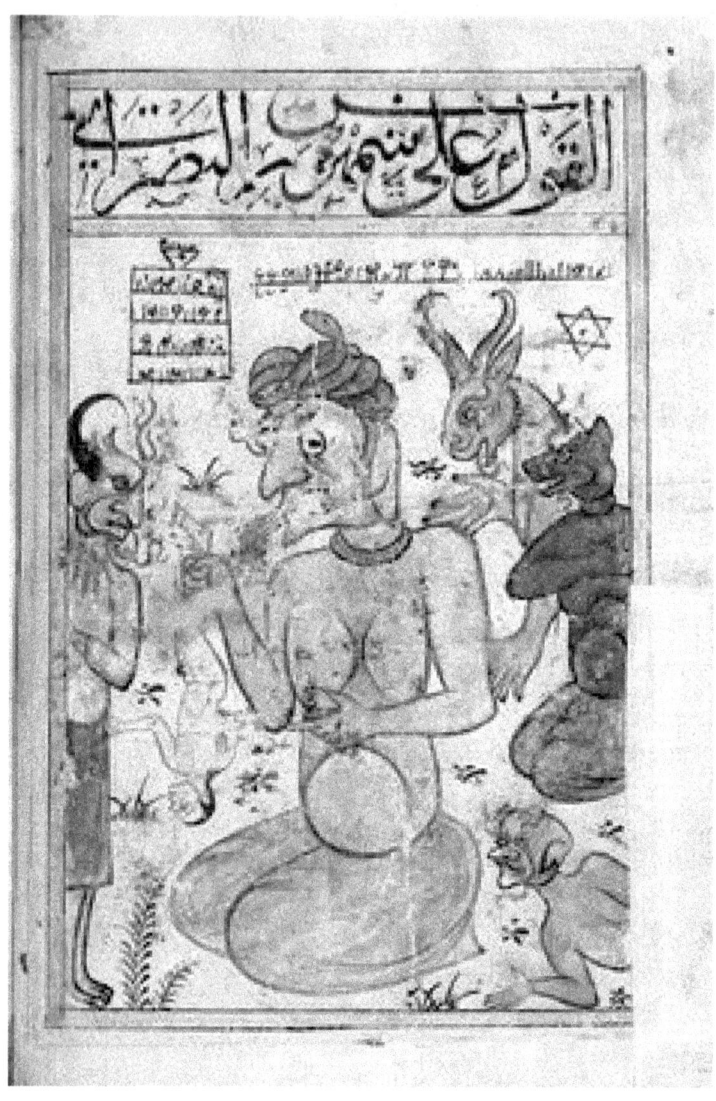

THE BLACK PATH

Sidi Chamharouch is usually one of the last of the Jilala family of *djinn* to be called. He is a very regal spirit, and arrives garbed in white. Chamharouch is considered to be the king (sultan) of this family of spirits, and is also one of the most deeply learned of the *djinn*. He is counted along the Muslim *djinn*, although Cheikh Azzeddine insists that he is to be paid cult when possible. Chamharouch is depicted as carrying books and scrolls like a scholar (despite his regal title), and is said to be able to pass on much occult and hidden knowledge to those who call him.

When Chamharouch is called, it is tradition to raise white banners, and a white cloth must be draped over the offering table. It is tradition to also place dates and milk on the table before or during his chant. If possession takes place, his *mluk* will expect to consume these offerings, and it can be dangerous if they are not present. He is especially likely to appear on Thursdays, which are said to be his day of the week.

His traditional chant is as follows:

Mokaddeme: 'Sidi Chamharouch, smahli'na!' (x2)

Chorus: 'Ya Sidi, smahli'na!' (x2)

Mokaddeme: 'Sidi Chamharouch, smahli'na!' (x2)

Chorus: 'Ya Moulay, smahli'na.' (x2)

Mokaddeme: 'Sidi Chamharouch, nta mul hurouf.' (x2)

Chorus: 'Sidi Chamharouch, nta ma'llem.' (x2)

Mokaddeme: 'Moulay, nta sultan l-aghwal' (x2)

Chorus: 'Moulay, nta sultan dyelna' (x2)

(ENGLISH TRANSLATION)

Mokademme: 'Sidi Chamharouch, bless us' (x2)

Chorus: 'Oh Saint, bless us' (x2)

Mokademme: 'Sidi Chamharouch, forgive us' (x2)

Chorus: 'Oh Master, forgive us' (x2)

Mokademme: 'Sidi Chamharouch, you're the lord of letters.' (x2)

Chorus: 'Sidi Chamharouch, you're a teacher.' (x2)

Mokademme: 'Master, you're the king of the *ghuls*.' (x2)

Chorus: 'Master, you're our master.' (x2)

THE BLACK PATH
BABA MIMOUN (Gnaoua family)

THE BLACK PATH

Baba Mimoun belongs to the *djinn* native to West Africa, and is said to have entered the North when the great slave armies came north from Mali under the Sultan Moulay Ismail. Baba Mimoun is depicted as an avuncular West African of dark complexion, and is the head of the *djinn* known as *el-kuhal* (the black) or *es'smara* (the tanned). He is sometimes arrayed in Malian or Senegalese clothing and wears a great black turban. Baba Mimoun is elderly and sometimes wields a great cane or walking staff. He is the patron of doorways and travelling, and his arrival is a good omen for the summoning of other *djinn*. People may seek his favor if they are about to take a journey, or have dealings that are directly related to farming, and also to Africa.

Black banners should be flown before his chant is recited, and the offering table should be covered with a black drape or cloth. When Baba Mimoun arrives, it is good to offer fresh dates and sweetened black coffee, which should already be present on the table.

His traditional chant is as follows:

Mokademme: 'Ya gnaoui Baba Mimun (x 3), mul bouab.'

Chorus: 'Ya gnaoui Baba Mimun (x 3), mul bouab.'

Mokademme: 'Nta gnaoui li 'andu tarbush dyel nur' (x2)

THE BLACK PATH

Chorus: 'Nta gnaoui li 'andu tarbush dyel nur' (x2)

Mokademme: 'Salaam Mimoun, mul treq!' (x 2)

Chorus: 'Salaam moulay, mul feleh' (x 2)

Mokademme: 'Salaam moulay, mul feleh' (x 2)

Chorus: 'Nta li jitii fi leil.' (x 2)

Mokademme: 'Sami Allah li man hamida.'

Chorus: 'Sami Allah li man hamida.'

Mokademme: 'Slah, slaam, ala rasoolu Llah.'

Chorus: 'Slah, slaam, ala rasoolu Llah.'

(ENGLISH TRANSLATION)

Mokademme: 'Oh gnaoui Baba Mimun (x 3), guardian of the doorways.'

Chorus: 'Oh gnaoui Baba Mimun (x 3), guardian of the doorways.'

THE BLACK PATH

Mokademme: 'You are the gnaoui with the bright shining cap' (x2)

Chorus: 'You are the gnaoui with the bright shining cap' (x2)

Mokademme: 'Welcome Mimoun, master of the ways!' (x 2)

Chorus: 'Welcome, master of the fields' (x 2)

Mokademme: 'Welcome, master of the fields' (x 2)

Chorus: ''You who arrive at night.' (x 2)

Mokademme: 'O Allah, Our Lord, hear our prayers.'

Chorus: 'O Allah, Our Lord, hear our prayers.'

Mokademme: 'Allah's peace on our master.'

Chorus: 'Allah's peace on our master.'

THE BLACK PATH
LALA MALIKA (Arabiya family)

Lala Malika ('Lady Malika') is much beloved by all. She is the most human of the *djinn*, and is very fond of all mortals. Lala Malika especially likes French culture and is known to cause her *mluk* to speak French, even if they do not know the language. This can be very disconcerting to observers who witness her possess someone for the first time. Lala Malika is very seductive, and enjoys flirting and sporting with men – her nocturnal visits tend to come in dreams, and are rarely harmful. She tends to possess attractive women, so as to better entice men. Possession by Lala Malika is said to enhance female fertility, and women who are having difficulty in conceiving are said to invite possession by her, in order to become pregnant.

Lala Malika enjoys silks and perfumes, and these must be present on the offering table. Perfume may be incensed into the air, to facilitate her arrival. She is also fond of smoking Marlboro cigarettes, and may request these as soon as she possesses a *murid*a.

The traditional chant to call her is as follows, and it is performed in French or Arabic:

Mokademme: 'Salaam Lalla Malika! Salaam ya fessiyya!'

Chorus: 'Salaam Lalla Malika! Salaam ya fessiyya!'

Mokademme: 'Salaam Lalla Malika, ala salamtik!'

THE BLACK PATH

Chorus: '*Salaam Lalla Malika, ala salamtik!*'

Mokademme: '*Allah! A Lalla Malika! Ismahni Lalla Malika!*'

Chorus: '*Allah! A Lalla Malika! Ismahni Lalla Malika!*'

Mokademme: '*Allah! Lalla Malika! Man 'ait 'aliha ma khafsh!*'

Chorus: '*Allah! Lalla Malika! Man 'ait 'aliha ma khafsh!*'

Mokademme: '*Allah! Bint an'nabi!*' *(x 2)*

Chorus: '*Allah! Bint an'nabi!*' *(x 2)*

(ENGLISH TRANSLATION)

Mokademme: 'Welcome Lalla Malika! Welcome, Lady of Fes!'

Chorus: 'Welcome, Lalla Malika! Welcome, Lady of Fes!'

Mokademme: 'Welcome Lalla Malika, well met!'

Chorus: 'Welcome Lalla Malika, well met!'

Mokademme: 'Oh Allah! Oh Lalla Malika! Hear us, Lalla Malika!'

Chorus: 'Oh Allah! Oh Lalla Malika! Hear us, Lalla Malika!'

Mokademme: 'Oh Allah! Oh Lalla Malika! Whoever calls you need not fear!'

Chorus: 'Oh Allah! Oh Lalla Malika! Whoever calls you need not fear!'

Mokademme: 'Oh Allah! Oh daughter of the prophet!' (x 2)

Chorus: 'Oh Allah! Oh daughter of the prophet!' (x 2)

THE BLACK PATH
LALA AICHA (Arabiyya family)

Lala Aicha Kandicha is the most notorious of the *djinn* in North Africa. Cheikh Azzeddine holds that she is the same spirit as Eiseth Kadesha, one of the wives of the fallen angel Samael, in the traditional tales of the Sephardic (Andalusian) Jews and was imported in the time of the Roman Empire. Others have stated that Aicha is a Berber version of Phoenician Astarte or Allat (Ereshkigal). Whatever her origins, Lala Aicha ('Lady Aicha') is feared and loved across the entire region. She is loved by women as a defender of the female gender, and is viciously protective of her female clients and devotees. Men fear her for her predatory sexuality: she is known to possess *murids* of both genders, and she is also known to appear visibly to her devotees in dreams and to seduce them. Men and women who fall prey to her sexual advances find themselves completely enthralled with her and become obedient to her every perverse whim. Men who 'marry' her enjoy her presence by night, but she is insatiable and steals the life essence of her husbands, reducing them to sexless husks over time. She is a cannibal spirit, and is known to attack lone travelers. She is said to have a fondness for devouring children, and many North African families will use her as a way of threatening children, saying (e.g.) 'Lala Aicha takes naughty children away in the night!'

The rituals that involve her are unique, in that not only are black flags flown and black cloth thrown across the offering table, but her rituals must be performed in near total darkness. In order to appease her, it is necessary that blood sacrifice be offered to her immediately on arrival, or during the chant. This should be of a black animal (goats, sheep are common), or else the blood of the devotees (less common).

Her traditional chant is as follows, and is performed largely by the *Mokademme*, together with rhythmic drumming:

Mokademme: '*A Lala 'Aicha! Aji wa kuni f'khidmat 'Llah wa*

rasoolu. Ya rab, slah ou slaam ala rasoolu 'Llah! Slaam, ya

Lalla 'Aicha!

Kulchi haadir, ya Lalla Aicha!

Ya Gnaouiyya! Ya Sudaniyya! O Hamduchiyya!

'Aicha jiit wa katsiin l-henna!

Salaam, ya bint l-wed.

Allah! Allah! Lalla Aicha!'

THE BLACK PATH
(ENGLISH TRANSLATION)

Mokademme: 'Oh Lady Aicha! Come and present yourself to the service of God and the Prophet.

Oh Lord, peace and blessings upon your messenger!

Welcome, Lady Aicha!

Everything is prepared, oh Lady Aicha!

Hey Gnaoui girl, hey Sudani girl, hey Hamduchi girl!

Aicha has come and awaits the henna!

Welcome, daughter of the river!

Allah! Allah! Lalla Aicha!'

At this point, Lala Aicha is likely to arrive. The lights should all be extinguished, save for one or two candles to give faint illumination. Cries and howls and ululations are expected from the chorus, especially from the female clients and *murids*. Wild dancing may ensue, and violently sexual possession may occur. Male as well as female *murids* and clients may experience possession, in either case they will exhibit very provocative behavior.

Intensive drumming is required to keep the *djinna* pleased. In regions outside of North Africa, it may be acceptable to play music suitable for dancing, as Lala Aicha is especially fond of dance.

While the drumming and dancing occurs, the *mokaddeme* and chorus shout the following again and again:

Mokademme: 'Hiya jaat, hiya jaat, hiya jaat Lalla Aicha!'

Chorus: 'Ya Allah! Ya Khaaliqna!'

(ENGLISH TRANSLATION)

Mokademme: 'She is come, she is come, Lala Aicha has come!!'

Chorus: 'Oh Allah! Our Protector!

The chanting and drumming must continue until Lala Aicha departs, at which point the *zaouia* or *Lila* space can be illuminated again. This *djinna* is especially dangerous, and must be placated immediately if there is any indication that she is displeased.

THE BLACK PATH

CHAPTER FOUR: REVELATIONS

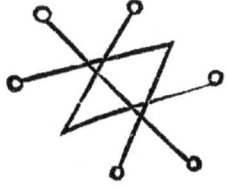

THE BLACK PATH

(This chapter provides an overview of the apocalyptic vision of Cheikh Azzeddine. The figure of the *Dajjal* (messiah) is treated, along with preparations for the coming final battle.)

Before the End, Allah will wax very proud. As the faith of the Nasrani (Christians) and the Muslims covers the earth, they will extinguish the other faiths. They will make war on each other, and commit many acts of desperate violence. Terrible weapons will be used, and the Earth will be stained with sickness and disease thereby. There will be drought and storms and earthquakes, and this will cause shortage of food and water. For this reason, the wise will make great store of supplies against that day. You should prepare dwellings for yourselves away from the great cities, and engage in tillage and livestock. Dig wells and find springs, that you will not be trapped when the dark times come.

The Shaitan, He will come himself before the Great Battle. In truth, He is already here within us. If you receive the Secret, then you have the essence of the Shaitan within you. He will never leave you or part from you, because you are precious to Him. All the universe is precious to Him, and He will not rest until it has been pulled down into the darkness of the Absolute, dissolved into its subtle parts. But the Shaitan will come, and He will cause a special prophet to be born. There will be two *murids*, a male and female, and they will be very close to the Shaitan. They will conceive a special child, and the essence of the Shaitan will enter into the foetus in the womb. It is not like you or me – we have to strive to attain the Secret, but this child be will be Secret made flesh. He will be golden skinned or golden haired, so he will be called the *Dajjal* (Arabic for golden). He will be the living representation of the Shaitan in this world. He will make great changes, and he will not come alone. When he comes, the Shaitain in flesh, he will send out a great call, and the chosen will hear it. If you are and I are alive, we will hear it. It will not be a call that is heard with the flesh, or the spirit, but the beast (*wahsh*) will hear the call. This is why I tell you now to begin to listen to the beast, so that you can hear the Shaitan when He calls for you.

When the Shaitan comes, there will be signs and wonders. He will have powers to do miracles like the prophets. At first His following will be small, but it will grow. Many will believe, and they will put their faith in Him. He will require people to receive His mark, and they will take it on their hands and their foreheads. When one of His chosen sees another, they will know each other. It will not be a visble mark, but a mark that can only be seen with the eyes of the heart. So you must learn to see with the eyes of the heart. When the *Dajjal* comes, He will kiss His companions (sahaba) on the face, and thereafter their face will have a sweet musk, like perfume. He will bring justice and power to the strong, and He will bring terrible wrath against His enemies.

The *Dajjal* will become the head of state of a great nation, with excellent science and weapons. Under his reign, the industries will flourish. In that day, resources will be very scare, and so the *Dajjal* will arm his military with new devices, and they will take possession of the lands of their enemies. He will set his eyes on Mecca and Medina, and he will invade those lands to take their gold. He will demolish the Kaaba, and in its place, he will build a great temple to the Taghut. He will compel the Quraish to beseech Allat, Manat, and Al-Uzza for mercy. Those who refuse will be sawn in half, like rotten wood. He will grant clemency to those who take bay'ah with him.

He will not enter Israel, for that nation will already be fallen to the Black Flags. Instead, he will turn his sights to the Far East. He will go to the wall of Dhul Qarnayn, and he will pull it down, so that Juj and Majuj are free to conquer China. The *Dajjal* will allow them to roam freely, and they will serve him utterly. In his time, the *djinn* and mala'ika will descend visibly. They will take humans for partners, and many strange children will be born to them. Science and witchcraft will flourish, and in that day, man shall look to the stars. Horrors will waken then and stalk among the ruins, and it will be good.

Then the *Dajjal* to speak to his sahaba (companions) about journeying to the stars, and about the doorways to the Absolute. Then they will build vessels for long journeys, and will seek the Void of space. Doorways will be built, so that a man can walk freely into the *akhira* (otherworld). People will curse death, and their learned will find ways to cheat it. The strong will prey on the weak, and devour their strength. In that day, the weak will be harvested like grain. No longer will man's years be three-score and ten, but ninety-nine times nine.

Then will strange signs and wonders appear in the heavens, which will show that the Light (*An'Nur*) is wroth and seeks to make war. The angels of the Light will descend to 'Arda (Earth), and the Taghut will descend, and there will be a great battle on the Mount of Olives. The Light will struggle against the Dark, and it will fail in that battle. There will be other battles, and many will perish who otherwise would have lived long. The Messiah will return then to l-Qods for the last battle, and he will have great power in his hands. But it will not avail him – the *Dajjal* shall find him and kill him with his bare hands. He will cut off the Messiah's head, and have his body thrown to the dogs. His (the *Dajjal*'s) enemies will be driven into hiding, and they shall be hunted for sport.

Then the *Dajjal* will set up his throne in the North, and he shall rule them all with an iron scepter. He shall have lordship and dominion until the very End. Then will the Absolute come, when the sun and stars die, and the seas murmur, and all the faithful will know eternal peace and glory, for ever and ever.

THE BLACK PATH

THE BLACK PATH

Photo credits:

The following images are obtained via Google Images, under Creative Commons License. The original photographers/artists are in no way connected with this work.

Cover image: Chris Parker via: < https://www.flickr.com/photos/-chrisparker2012/14963313385/>

Inside Cover image: Christopher L. via <https://www.flickr.com/photos-/toffiundkamera/8577356094/>

p. 11: < https://commons.wikimedia.org/wiki/File:Zaouia_el_hadj_-ahmed_ou_boubiche_ben_mohamed_azaroual_chikh_tisakifin_tijdad_bouzina.jpg>

p.13: < http://www.abc.net.au/news/2013-08-22/soay-ram/4904780>

p. 20: < https://commons.wikimedia.org/wiki/File:-Tuareg2.JPG>

p. 25: < http://photos1.blogger.com/blogger/1759/1777/400/sufi02.jpg>

p.54: < https://s-media-cache-ak0.pinimg.com/236x/e9/1c/c1/-e91cc17415ae9aca72032269b7fa89a1.jpg>

p. 135: <http://res.freestockphotos.biz/pictures/12/12114-illustration-of-a-skull-and-crossbones-pv.png>

p.138: < https://www.flickr.com/photos/wackelijmrooster/-3826568966>

p.141: < https://upload.wikimedia.org/wikipedia-/commons-/9/9a/-Mali1974-151_hg.jpg>

p.149: < https://en.wikipedia.org/wiki/File:Looking_up_at_a_standing_-naked_woman.jpg>

THE BLACK PATH

THE BLACK PATH

AZZEDDINI *TARIQA* CONTACT

tariqa@safe-mail.net

www.ingramcontent.com/pod-product-compliance
Lightning Source LLC
Chambersburg PA
CBHW060156050426
42446CB00013B/2848